THE CROSS OF JESUS CHRIST

ITS MESSAGE AND POWER

Chukwugoziam Onianwah

Copyright © 2018 Chukwugoziam Onianwah.

All rights reserved. No part of this book may be reproduced, stored, or transmitted by any means—whether auditory, graphic, mechanical, or electronic—without written permission of the author, except in the case of brief excerpts used in critical articles and reviews. Unauthorized reproduction of any part of this work is illegal and is punishable by law.

This book is a work of non-fiction. Unless otherwise noted, the author and the publisher make no explicit guarantees as to the accuracy of the information contained in this book and in some cases, names of people and places have been altered to protect their privacy.

Great Grace Publishing
13132 Shinnecock Drive
Silver Spring, Maryland, 20904 USA
Visit our Website at www.greatgracepublishing.com
Email: info@greatgraceinc.com

All Rights Reserved
Library of Congress Cataloging-in-Publication Data
Great Grace Publishing
The Cross of Jesus Christ: Its Message and Power
Chukwugoziam Onianwah
Includes Captions

ISBN: 978-0-9987461-1-1 (sc)
ISBN: 978-0-9987461-2-8 (hc)
ISBN: 978-0-9987461-3-5 (e)

Library of Congress Control Number: 2018902645

1. Religious – Evangelism – Faith – 1. Title

Cover Design & Contents Page Design by Great Grace Publishing Inc.
Published in Silver Spring MD by Great Grace.
A registered trademark of Great Grace Inc.

Because of the dynamic nature of the Internet, any web addresses or links contained in this book may have changed since publication and may no longer be valid. The views expressed in this work are solely those of the author and do not necessarily reflect the views of the publisher, and the publisher hereby disclaims any responsibility for them.

Any people depicted in stock imagery provided by Getty Images are models, and such images are being used for illustrative purposes only.
Certain stock imagery © Getty Images.

rev. date: 06/12/2018

Unless otherwise stated, all scripture taken from the King James Version of the Bible.

Scripture quotations marked (NIV) are taken from the Holy Bible, New International Version®, NIV®. Copyright © 1973, 1978, 1984, 2011 by Biblica, Inc.™ Used by permission of Zondervan. All rights reserved worldwide. www.zondervan.com The "NIV" and "New International Version" are trademarks registered in the United States Patent and Trademark Office by Biblica, Inc.™

Scripture quotations marked (AMP) are taken from the Amplified Bible, Copyright © 1954, 1958, 1962, 1964, 1965, 1987 by The Lockman Foundation. Used by permission.

Scripture taken from the New King James Version®. Copyright © 1982 by Thomas Nelson. Used by permission. All rights reserved.

Scripture quotations marked (NLT) are taken from the Holy Bible, New Living Translation, copyright ©1996, 2004, 2015 by Tyndale House Foundation. Used by permission of Tyndale House Publishers, Inc., Carol Stream, Illinois 60188. All rights reserved.

Scripture quotations marked (TLB) are taken from The Living Bible copyright © 1971. Used by permission of Tyndale House Publishers, Inc., Carol Stream, Illinois 60188. All rights reserved.

Scripture quotations taken from the New American Standard Bible® (NASB), Copyright © 1960, 1962, 1963, 1968, 1971, 1972, 1973, 1975, 1977, 1995 by The Lockman Foundation Used by permission. www.Lockman.org

CONTENTS

Foreword ix
Commendations xiii
Acknowledgements xv
Introduction xvii

1. Who is Jesus Christ? 1
   When Deity Visits Humanity 7
   Why His Death on the Cross was Necessary 8
2. What is the Cross of Jesus Christ? 11
   Why God Rejected Jesus 16
   The Power of Love 20
   What caused Paul to change so dramatically? 23
   The Gift of Hope 30
3. What is the Significance of the Cross? 32
   The Miracles on the Cross 34
   How to Gain Access to the Throne of Grace 39
   How to Influence Political Leaders 42
4. What is the Message of the Cross? 45
   How the Cross Can Change Lives 46
   How Jesus Destroyed the Works of the Devil 52
5. What is the Power of the Cross? 69
   How to Win the Fight Against Sin 73
   How the Spiritual Realm Controls the Physical Realm 75
   How do I gain from these things? 82
   How to Use the Power of Jesus' Name 83
6. How Can You Claim the Power of the Cross? 93
   Steps to Salvation 94
   Prayer for Salvation 96

FOREWORD

Many have read and have heard about the cross on which Jesus died. A large number of Christians celebrate Easter by recalling the sufferings Jesus went through on the cross.

However, not many know some of the spiritual dimensions of the sufferings. Not many know why Jesus had to die, why the death had to be on the cross and no other way.

A number of converts have joined the faith through open crusades, house to house or one on one Evangelism, regular Sunday morning or evening services, street Evangelism etc. where the gospel message was preached yet not many have actually come to realize the tremendous power the cross of Jesus Christ has nor have they come to understand that it has a message for every human being on this planet earth.

A number of people both Christians and non-Christians know and can quote John 3:16 but not many have realized that the cross is the place where this love of God was demonstrated as Jesus hung on it.

Holding the view that the cross of Jesus Christ is the single most important event in the history of humanity, the writer wants as many people as possible to know and experience this powerful truth

In this book, The Cross Of Jesus Christ: It's Message & Power, the author takes the reader through a deep dive into scriptures to bring to the surface some truths about the Incarnation, sufferings, death (by crucifixion) and resurrection of Jesus Christ. He went further beyond the physical to look at the spiritual dimensions of the events on the cross of Jesus Christ and bring out their importance and blessings to mankind.

Starting with a chapter on who Jesus is, why he had to come bodily as a human being, why God the Father rejected him, why he had to die on the cross etc. As you read, you come face to face with the fact that the cross is not only a demonstration of love but it carries a message for everyone: that on the cross, God demonstrated His love for mankind when He (in Christ Jesus) took away our sin with all the consequences that sin carries.

The cross carries power (that can be activated) and is available to anyone who will hear, receive and take the necessary steps outlined in the book.

Finally, in this book, the writer presents a thorough exposition of the gospel message, equips the reader with insights into what Jesus did in order for them to be saved as well as equip the believer in Christ with requisite information in order to share their faith in Christ with others.

I believe you will find the book interesting as you read.

Pastor Johnson Odesola
AGO Admin. RCCG.

DEDICATION

To Jesus Christ, who gave himself for me and saved my soul.

COMMENDATIONS

We have known **Pastor Chukwugoziam Onianwah** as a child of God and among the best Christian examples seen in our time.

The Book, "***The Cross of Jesus Christ Its Message and Power***", to us, is a masterpiece from a great mind written to encourage and strengthen believers.

The Cross of Jesus Christ is exalted by Apostle Paul as the central theme of the proclamation of the gospel. The message of the Cross though simple and ordinary, yet was not so simple as to lack in thoroughness and thought. Apostle Paul's declaration in 1 Cor. 1:17 is not done with wisdom and eloquence of men which would have emptied the power of the Cross.

Today, many people use the cross in different ways that may not show how dreadful the cross used to be. The cross was an instrument of death; death for notorious criminals. The cross was an instrument of immense suffering. The victim of the cross was fastened by nail or rope with arms outstretched.

The author; in this book, is not talking about different types of cross, as there are indeed many types of cross. The Book takes us through the journey of the Redemptive work of the Messiah; the transaction that took place, the rejection, the miracles, the freedom from sin, the reconciliation, forgiveness and adoption; all these happened on the Cross of Calvary.

We agree with the author in the introduction that: "*there is no salvation without the Cross of Christ*".

This Book is therefore recommended to both the ordained and lay regardless of denomination. To God be the glory!

The Most Rev. Dr. Ignatius C.O. Kattey (JP)
Dean Church of Nigeria
Archbishop, Province of Niger Delta,
Bishop Diocese of Niger Delta North &
Grand Patron, Scripture Union (Nigeria).

The cross of Jesus Christ continues to remain at the center of Christianity. Jesus invites us to understand the power and message of the cross when he said: 'just as Moses lifted up the serpent in the wilderness, so must the Son of Man be lifted up, that whoever believes in him may have eternal life.'

In this book, Rev. Chukwugoziam Onianwah unravels the power and message of the cross all anew. It is a rallying call on contemporary Christians who loathsomely reject the cross and its varied implications as 'not their portion'. The story of the cross which this book highlights forewarns us all that God's glory comes not by going around the dark valley, but through it. I recommend this book to all pastors and their congregations and to all who are seeking to understand the meaning and power of the cross of Jesus Christ.

Rev. Msgr. PIUS KII, Ph.D
Department of Canon Law
Catholic Institute of West Africa

ACKNOWLEDGEMENTS

We thank the Father, Son, and Holy Spirit for the work of the Trinity in our salvation through the sacrifice of Jesus Christ, the Son of God. We are grateful for the Grace and call of God on our lives and for giving us a part of the ministry.

Special thanks go to Sister Nancy Shoptaw for her professionalism in painstakingly preparing the manuscript and transforming it into what you have in your hands. Much appreciation goes to my friend and pastor, Professor Nimi Wariboko for his helpful insights, thoughts, and suggestions toward broadening the manuscript to give it global appeal. Thank you to my young friend Edodi Sampson for his assistance on this labor-of-love project. Finally, much gratitude goes to my wife for all her prayers and support at all times, including taking care of our young men, Isaac and David, while daddy was busy.

INTRODUCTION

There have been many important events in the history of man. Examples of some of these positive events that are substantiated with scientific backgrounds include: man's first landing on the moon, the Wright brothers' first airplane flight, Alexander Fleming's discovery of penicillin, and man's ability to conduct electricity. Other events, such as the terrorist attack widely referred to as 9/11, have no equal in terms of evil.

However, considering the eternal destiny of man, the cross is the most important and significant of all events in the history of humanity—past, present, and future all put together. This book will highlight some of the reasons we hold this to be true.

In 1 Corinthians 1:17–18, the word of God says,

> Christ sent me . . . to preach the gospel: not with wisdom of words, lest the cross of Christ should be made of none effect. For the preaching of the cross is to them that perish foolishness; but unto us which are saved it is the power of God.

This text clearly shows that there is what is referred to as the cross of Christ. The cross of Christ exists and it holds the power of God for those who believe. We can trust what the Bible says; we can claim it as truth. While 1 Corinthians portrays this most important and significant historical event as "the cross of Christ," John 19:25 describes it as the "cross of Jesus."

> Now there stood by the cross of Jesus, his mother, and his mother's sister, Mary the wife of Cleophas, and Mary Magdalene.

In the same manner, John 19:30 establishes that Jesus died on the cross.

> When Jesus therefore had received the vinegar, he said, It is finished: and he bowed his head, and gave up the ghost.

If we look back at the first book of the New Testament, in Matthew 27:40 we read that people saw Jesus on the cross and that some made a mockery of him. "And saying, Thou that destroyest the temple, and buildest it in three days, save thyself. If thou be the Son of God, come down from the cross." Similarly, in verse 42, some looked at him on the cross and taunted him. "He saved others; himself he cannot save. If he be the King of Israel, let him now come down from the cross, and we will believe him."

From these passages of scripture, we can establish that Jesus Christ died on the cross. This death on the cross (together with his resurrection on the third day) is the gospel message.

> Moreover, brethren, I declare unto you the gospel which I preached unto you, which also ye have received, and wherein ye stand; By which also ye are saved, if ye keep in memory what I preached unto you, unless ye have believed in vain. For I delivered unto you first of all that which I also received, how that Christ died for our sins according to the scriptures; And that he was buried, and that he rose again the third day according to the scriptures. (1 Cor 15:1–4)

The gospel message is made up of the death, burial, and resurrection of Jesus Christ according to this scripture above. However, this book focuses on the events that took place on the cross leading up to his death, hence the cross of Jesus Christ. Through the above scriptures we have established that there is a cross of Christ and that this cross has a message. This message is given to every believer in Christ to proclaim. Every believer has a mandate to preach the gospel to every creature. Mark 16:15 says, "And he said unto them, Go ye into all the world, and preach the gospel to every creature." To preach is to announce, proclaim, or tell.

This book intends to look at the gospel message and the significance of the cross of Christ to the whole world. The gospel is the message of redemption in Christ through faith in his death, burial, and resurrection. This redemption comes through faith in Jesus Christ alone. Thus, some of the questions we will answer include: What is the gospel message? What is the cross of Christ? What does the cross of Christ mean both literally and spiritually? What happened on that cross and what does it mean for the human race? What is the power of the cross of Christ? How do I appropriate and benefit from the power of the cross of Christ?

Redemption, salvation, forgiveness of sins, and reconciliation with God (after the separation that took place in the garden of Eden) are available to all mankind only because of Jesus' sacrificial death on the cross.

> For there is none other name under heaven given among men, whereby we must be saved. (Acts 4:12)
>
> In whom [Jesus] we have redemption through his blood, *even* the forgiveness of sins. (Col 1:14)
>
> Jesus saith . . ., I am the way, the truth, and the life: no man cometh unto the Father, but by me. (John 14:6)

In other words, there is no salvation without the cross of Christ, and Jesus makes this clear. Many people may disagree with this statement as some have said Jesus cannot be the only way to God. They cite other religions and religious leaders as pathways to God. But the scriptures quoted above are what the Bible declares and we affirm the Bible to be true. Instead of wrestling with this statement, as many do—and still wrestle to believe even at the point of death—why gamble until it may be too late to take a risk? Why wait to die in order to find out who was right? Today, do not harden your heart; choose to hear his voice, because Hebrews 9:27 says, "It is appointed unto men once to die, but after this the judgment." Death is something every human being will face one day, sooner or later. Death is inevitable. And after death, there is judgment.

Dear reader, how prepared are you for death and the judgment that will follow? Have you heard about Jesus and what he did on the cross? As you read, may you experience that power in Jesus' name.

Chapter 1

WHO IS JESUS CHRIST?

Today we will answer two important questions: Who is Jesus Christ and why is his death on the cross so important for the entire human race? The answer you hear to this question depends on who you ask, as different people have different ideas and opinions about who Jesus is. When Jesus was here physically (in the flesh) and asked his disciples, the men who had been accompanying him for awhile, he got different answers and they are recorded in Matthew 16:13–18 (NIV).

> When Jesus came to the region of Caesarea Philippi, he asked his disciples, "Who do people say the Son of Man is?" They replied, "Some say John the Baptist; others say Elijah; and still others, Jeremiah or one of the prophets." "But what about you?" he asked. "Who do you say I am?" Simon Peter answered, "You are the Messiah, the Son of the living God." Jesus replied, "Blessed are you, Simon son of Jonah, for this was not revealed to you by flesh and blood, but by my Father in heaven. And I tell you that you are Peter, and on this rock I will build my church, and the gates of Hades will not overcome it."

From the answer Peter gave, identifying Jesus as the Messiah even though no one had ever told him that, and the comment Jesus made, saying the information came from the Father, we conclude that the answer to the question requires some measure of divine assistance or, simply put, we know the answer by divine revelation. Luke 10:22 says,

"All things are delivered to me of my Father: and no man knoweth who the Son is, but the Father; and who the Father is, but the Son, and *he* to whom the Son will reveal *him*."

But what does the Bible say about who Jesus is? Many in history and even as recorded in the Bible have found it difficult to simply accept what the Bible plainly says about who Jesus is, as we shall see shortly.

In John 1:1 we are told, "In the beginning was the Word, and the Word was with God, and the Word was God." If we stop at this first verse, the Bible says the Word was God. Who did the Bible refer to here? The Word. Observe that the two, God and his Word, were together from the beginning.

Next question: Who is the Word? If we continue to read chapter 1 up to verse 18, we discover a number of truths, including that the Word created all things. Most people believe that God created the world. Some say a being somewhere created it, while others describe that being as a power or a force. But many hold the belief that there is a creator (God) somewhere who created the world. Here, the Bible says the Word created all things, and so we are back to our original question: Who is the Word? Revelation 19:11–13 addresses this question by revealing what the disciple John witnessed when heaven opened up and he saw Jesus.

> And I saw heaven opened, and behold a white horse; and he that sat upon him was called Faithful and True, and in righteousness he doth judge and make war. His eyes were as a flame of fire, and on his head were many crowns; and he had a name written, that no man knew, but he himself. And he was clothed with a vesture dipped in blood: and his name is called The Word of God.

Verse 13, talking about Jesus, says, "his name is called The Word of God." Further, as we turn back to the book of John we read, "In him was life" (1:4). Again, a number of people hold the belief that God is the source of life, and they are right. But we also learn here in the book of John that in Jesus is life. Verse 10 says, "He was in the world, and the world was made by him, and the world knew him not."

The world was made by him. This statement is reinforced in the Bible several times. Colossians 1:16 says, "For by him were all things created, that are in heaven, that are in earth, visible and invisible, whether they be thrones, or dominions, or principalities or powers: all things were created by him and for him." If we back up to verse 14, it becomes very clear that this passage is talking about Jesus when it declares that he created all things. Furthermore, John 1:12 says, "But as many as received him, to them gave he power to become the sons of God, *even* to them that believe on his name." You cannot give what you do not have, and so for him to give the right to become a son of God to everyone who believes in him shows that he has that power or right. As we continue reading the first chapter of John, verse 14 says, "And the Word was made flesh, and dwelt among us, (and we beheld his glory, the glory as of the only begotten of the Father,) full of grace and truth." Jesus walked upon this earth in the flesh, as a man.

But the Word is Spirit. We learn in John 6:63 that "It is the spirit that quickeneth; the flesh profiteth nothing: the words that I speak unto you, they are spirit, and they are life." But also that God is a Spirit: "God is a Spirit: and they that worship him must worship him in spirit and in truth" (4:24). How then did Word (Spirit) become flesh? As spirits cannot inhabit the natural world the way they are, they require a body in which to live and function in this natural physical habitat. So God, in his wisdom, chose to create this physical habitat so that his plan for mankind could be carried out. Hebrews 10:5–10 shows us how he did this.

> Wherefore when he cometh into the world, he saith, Sacrifice and offering thou wouldest not, but a body hast thou prepared me: In burnt offerings and sacrifices for sin thou hast had no pleasure. Then said I, Lo, I come (in the volume of the book it is written of me,) to do thy will, O God. Above when he said, Sacrifice and offering and burnt offerings and offering for sin thou wouldest not, neither hadst pleasure therein; which are offered by the law; Then said he, Lo, I come to do thy will, O God. He taketh away the first, that he may establish the

second. By the which will we are sanctified through the offering of the body of Jesus Christ once for all.

God prepared a body for Jesus to dwell in in order to function on the earth when he came as a human being. If the body had dropped from heaven, it would not have qualified to be the human sacrifice. The body needed to be carried in the womb of a virgin and born in a natural birth process. The newborn child needed to be a human being, yet without the contamination of Adam's sin.

When it was time for Jesus to be born, God gave an angel a word to speak to a virgin, and as she believed (received) the word spoken to her by the angel, conception took place in her womb. Luke 1:26–28 (NLT) shares details of this immaculate conception. The angel Gabriel is sent by God to a virgin named Mary who is engaged to a man named Joseph, of the house of David (26–27). Gabriel's words were received by Mary in wonderment: "'Greetings, favored one! The Lord is with you.' But she was much perplexed by his words and pondered what sort of greeting this might be" (28–29). While wondering within herself, then came the words of comfort and promise, "Do not be afraid, Mary, for you have found favor with God. And now, you will conceive in your womb and bear a son, and you will call him Jesus" (30–31). Through the reading of these passages we are able to recognize that in the name "Jesus" comes the fulfillment of the ages.

Thus it is no wonder that Mary responds, "How can this be, since I am a virgin?" (34). The wonderful exchange between Mary and the angel Gabriel continues to express God's pure and simple gift to Mary. However, Mary's final response expresses the faith of the young mother and chosen one of God: "'Here am I, let it be with me according to your word.' Then the angel departed from her" (38).

Again, who is Jesus? Let us see what he said of himself and the result. Jesus wanted people to know who he was, where he came from, and that God had sent him for a purpose. When the Jews approached him in the temple, "Jesus said unto them, 'if God were your Father, ye would have loved me: for I proceeded forth and came from God; neither came I of myself, but he sent me'" (John 8:42 NLT).

I like the way Apostle Victor James put it while explaining this verse.

He said God came out of himself. Putting it that way means that God came out of himself and entered into this world while still in heaven on his throne. A man of God once described Jesus as God in the flesh (human form), and we now regularly hear this term. This is confirmed in 1 Timothy 3:16 where the scripture says, "And without controversy great is the mystery of godliness: God was manifested in the flesh, justified in the Spirit, seen by angels, preached among the Gentiles, believed on in the world, received up in glory."

In the book of John, Jesus further said of himself:

> I came forth from the Father, and am come into the world: again, I leave the world and go to the Father. (16:28)

> For the Father judgeth no man, but hath committed all judgment unto the Son: That all *men* should honour the Son, even as they honour the Father. He that honoureth not the Son honoureth not the Father which hath sent him. (5:22–23)

If Jesus were not God, men would be committing idolatry if they were to honor him in the same way they honor the Almighty God. But probably the boldest statement he made was when he said,

> I and my Father are one. (10:30)

When Jesus gave this mighty revelation, the truth was too heavy for the people to handle. They didn't understand and so were outraged and took up stones to stone him.

> Jesus answered them, many good works have I shewed you from my Father; for which of those works do ye stone me? The Jews answered him, saying, For a good work we stone thee not; but for blasphemy; and because that thou, being a man, makest thyself God. (32–33)

The Jews were saying, in other words, that if you say you and God are one, you are simply saying you are God. Why was this heavy for them? Because they fell back on the mental concept they had of God from the Old Testament days when God came down on Mount Sinai to visit them. Their perception of God was that of a very fearful invisible personality whose mere presence caused earthquakes, lightning, and thunder; and no one was allowed near where he was. We get a sense of God's wrath in Hebrews 12:18–21.

> For ye are not come unto the mount that might be touched, and that burned with fire, nor unto blackness, and darkness, and tempest, And the sound of a trumpet, and the voice of words; which voice they that heard entreated that the word should not be spoken to them any more: (For they could not endure that which was commanded, And if so much as a beast touch the mountain, it shall be stoned or thrust through with a dart: And so terrible was the sight, that Moses said I exceedingly fear and quake.)

Having that mental picture of how terrifying God's presence had been, imagine what mental and cultural shock it was to them when Jesus (who was with and seen of them) said he and the Father are one. Blasphemy of the highest order, they thought, and so reacted that way; they took up stones to stone him to death.

The story has not changed to date. Many find it hard to accept that Jesus is God, but he is. As we have learned from the Bible, which speaks the truth, the Word (Jesus) was God, He is one with God, he proceedeth forth, and came from God. First John 5:7 says, "There are three that bear record in Heaven, the Father, the Word and the Holy Ghost and the three are one."

This truth about Jesus being God cannot be reasoned out through the process of natural logic as it is beyond the natural logic of human reasoning. No man has ever known the truth of God through the process of natural reasoning. He is beyond human mental comprehension. St. Augustine (354–430 AD) understood this well when he said, *Credo ut intellegam*, "I believe in order that I may understand." One must first believe and then one is given understanding. You may not know God by volumes of books, but you can know him by personal encounters with him. The truth of God is believed with the heart. By believing in your heart that the Father, the Word, and the Holy Ghost are three that bear record in heaven and that these three are one, you are receiving the truth by faith. By believing in your heart that Jesus Christ is God, you are receiving the truth by faith. By believing in your heart that he can save you and give you eternal life, you are receiving the truth by faith. Believe that Jesus is God in the flesh, and that in him, deity comes to humanity. Wanting to reason this out logically may be likened to attempting to empty a river with a teaspoon. Thus, the truth about God is received with the heart and by faith only.

> And without controversy great is the mystery of godliness: God was manifest in the flesh, justified in the Spirit, seen of angels, preached unto the Gentiles, believed on in the world, received up into glory. (1 Tim 3:16)

Jesus who was God manifested in the flesh died on the cross for man's sins, was buried, and raised from the dead after three days.

WHEN DEITY VISITS HUMANITY

God designed, from time immemorial, that deity, in the person of Jesus, was coming to humanity in the flesh. Many prophets prophesied his coming and expectations were heightened. For example, Isaiah and some other Old Testament prophets prophesied his birth. Isaiah lets us know what to expect. "Therefore the LORD himself shall give you a sign; behold a virgin shall conceive, and bear a son, and shall call his name Immanuel" (7:14). Immanuel means "God with us." God with us means that God has come not just to put his hand on us, not just to say, "well done" and give us a pat on the back and push us forward. He has come to stay, he has come to dwell; he has come to reside with us!

Isaiah continues to share about the birth of Jesus, including his leadership position and characteristics. "For unto us a child is born, unto us a son is given: and the government shall be upon his shoulder: and his name shall be called Wonderful, Counsellor, The Mighty God, The everlasting Father, The Prince of Peace" (9:6). Two things are described here. Physically, a child is born. But more than that, a son is given. God gave us his Son or gave us of himself, as the two are one. For this we can be eternally grateful. "For God so loved the world, that he gave his only begotten Son, that whosoever believeth in him should not perish, but have everlasting life" (John 3:16). Micah 5:2 puts it another way: "But thou, Bethlehem Eph-ra-tah, though thou be little among the thousands of Judah, yet out of thee shall he come forth unto me that is to be ruler in Israel; whose goings forth have been of old, from everlasting." Note that the only one who has existed forever, from everlasting, is God.

Jesus' birth was not only prophesied many years before, but when it eventually happened, his birth was accompanied with signs such as angelic visitation and announcement, as we see in Luke 1:26–28. First, an angel announced his birth to some shepherds, and in the end all that they had seen and heard was carried out. If we review Luke 2:6–20, we learn that Mary has given birth to Jesus Christ.

> And so it was, that, while they were there, the days were accomplished that she should be delivered. (6)

All through the Bible, angels appeared to human beings only when there was very important or serious information to convey and this was not often.

WHY HIS DEATH ON THE CROSS WAS NECESSARY

The birth of Jesus was not only foretold but was accompanied by signs as well. And as much as his birth was ushered in with a number of signs, so was his death. Signs that confirm that deity died for man were undeniable upon Jesus' death. A total eclipse of the sun occurred and then an earthquake announced his death. Matthew 27:50–54 offers specific details surrounding the moment Jesus died.

> Jesus, when he had cried again with a loud voice, yielded up the ghost. And, behold, the veil of the temple was rent

in twain from the top to the bottom; and the earth did quake, and the rocks rent; And the graves were opened; and many bodies of the saints which slept arose, And came out of the graves after his resurrection, and went into the holy city, and appeared unto many. Now when the centurion, and they that were with him, watching Jesus, saw the earthquake, and those things that were done, they feared greatly, saying, Truly this was the Son of God.

Luke 23:44–47 provides his account of the series of events:

And it was about the sixth hour, and there was a darkness over all the earth until the ninth hour. And the sun was darkened, and the veil of the temple was rent in the midst. And when Jesus had cried with a loud voice, he said, Father, into thy hands I commend my spirit: and having said thus, he gave up the ghost. Now when the centurion saw what was done, he glorified God, saying, Certainly this was a righteous man.

God, in Christ, came as a human being to die for human beings. He had a purpose, to save mankind, and he carried out this purpose through the life, death, and as we will see in later chapters, the resurrection of Jesus. Romans 8:3 says, "For what the law could not do, in that it was weak through the flesh, God sending his own Son in the likeness of sinful flesh, and for sin, condemned sin in the flesh." In Hebrews 10:10–14 we are told that Jesus made the ultimate, forever sacrifice by dying on the cross.

His sacrifice was perfect, complete and enough for all time. By the which will we are sanctified through the offering of the body of Jesus Christ once for all. And every priest standeth daily ministering and offering oftentimes the same sacrifices, which can never take away sins: But this man, after he had offered one sacrifice for sins for ever, sat down on the right hand of God; From henceforth expecting till his enemies be made his footstool. For by one offering he hath perfected for ever them that are sanctified.

His death on the cross put an end to the problem sin posed to man from its beginning in the garden of Eden. Sin had stood between God and man as a barrier from the day Adam sinned in the garden. Once sin was introduced into the world, man could not approach God; rather, he ran away from God. Neither could God fellowship with man anymore as he did with Adam before sin came between them.

The sacrificial death on the cross is a symbol of the end of the consequences of sin, including death, as Jesus took it away, and those who believe in him have been redeemed from sin and death and now have eternal life. The death of Jesus Christ on the cross was not the first nor was it the last time a human being was crucified by hanging on the cross to die. So what made his own case so important and significant to the entire human race and history of man? Given that he died sacrificially for others, one thing that made his death so significant is that deity died for humanity: God in the flesh willingly laid down his life for his creatures. "Therefore doth my Father love me, because I lay down my life, that I might take it again. No man taketh it from me, but I lay it down of myself. I have power to lay it down, and I have power to take it again. This commandment have I received of my Father" (John 10:17–18). Furthermore, what that sacrificial death offers to mankind is what I believe makes it so important an event, and it matters what the intended beneficiaries of the sacrifice make of the offer.

Dear reader, what have you done with the information that Jesus suffered and died on the cross for you and for me? Remember, as many as received him, he gave the power to become the sons of God. Have you received him into your heart?

> Verily, verily, I say unto you, He that heareth my word, and believeth on Him that sent me, hath everlasting life, and shall not come into condemnation; but is passed from death unto life. (5:24)

Chapter 2

WHAT IS THE CROSS OF JESUS CHRIST?

The English word "cross" has many meanings: some are not related to Jesus and a number of meanings do relate to him and his death. According to M. G. Easton's *Illustrated Bible Dictionary*, the cross refers to the cross upon which Jesus died, the crucifixion of Jesus as the culmination of his redemptive mission, the teaching of redemption gained by Jesus' death, and the cross as the symbol of Christianity.[1] According to James Orr in the *International Standard Bible Encyclopedia*, no word in human language has become more universally known than "cross," which is

> derived from the Latin word *crux*. In the Greek language it is *stauros*, but sometimes we find the word *skolops* used as its Greek equivalent. The historical writers, who transferred the events of Roman history into the Greek language, make use of these two words. No word in human language has become more universally known than this word, and that because all of the history of the world since the death of Christ has been measured by the distance which separates events from it. The symbol and principal content of the Christian religion and of Christian civilization is found in this one word.[2]

---

[1] *Illustrated Bible Dictionary*, 3rd ed., s.v. "cross."
[2] *International Standard Bible Encyclopedia*, 1915 ed., s.v. "cross."

According to John McClintock and James Strong in the *McClintock and Strong Encyclopedia*, the cross "signifies properly the instrument of crucifixion; and hence (by metonymy) crucifixion itself, namely, that of Christ."[3]

In modern language, the cross is used to describe any suffering that a believer endures because of Jesus. Matthew 10:38 says, "And he that taketh not his cross, and followeth after me, is not worthy of me."

The cross is a structure generally made of wood that consists essentially of an upright and a transverse piece, used to execute persons in ancient times. Historically, death by crucifixion originated from the region of Persia, regions in present-day Iran and Iraq. This method of execution was copied, modified, and adopted by the Romans, and became the preferred choice for inflicting torture leading to death for criminals and political enemies.

What is the significance of the cross to the death of Jesus? We know that every human being has to die. "And as it is appointed unto men once to die, but after this the judgment" (Heb 9:27). It follows then that Jesus would have to die, but why on the cross and not some other way? After all, he could have died any other way, especially by stoning, which was the way Jews killed those sentenced to death in the Old Testament. Or, he could have died by scourging, which was fairly commonplace at the time of Jesus. Why did he die on the cross specifically? After all, if death is death, he could have died any of these other ways, and so why death by hanging on the cross? This question is even more significant when we realize from reading the Bible that Jesus was actually scourged first and that it was rare for anyone to be scourged and crucified for the same offense during his days.

Note that to crucify means to kill by nailing and hanging on a cross. The significance of the cross in the death of Jesus Christ will become clearer as we begin to witness the events and understand how they fit into God's plan.

The cross is an instrument used to execute those who were sentenced to death by hanging, and such hangings took place publicly. As an instrument of punishment, it is quite effective and was the method of choice for carrying out capital punishment in those days. Hanging

---

[3] *McClintock and Strong Encyclopedia*, 1981 reprint, s.v. "cross."

on a cross led to a slow and very painful death as the individuals were actually nailed to the cross so that they suffered intensely and died slowly, uncomfortably, and painfully.

Mostly, people punished in this manner were criminals, offenders that broke laws, and sometimes, political opponents. However, in the case of Jesus, he was neither a political enemy nor did he commit any offense or break any laws, neither human nor divine. Hebrews 4:15 reiterates Jesus' innocence.

> For we have not an high priest which cannot be touched with the feeling of our infirmities; but was in all points tempted like as we are, yet without sin.

Humanly speaking, the cross is the place where the sacrifice and death of the Son of God culminated. As the cross is also used to describe the totality of Jesus' sufferings for humanity, the nailing and hanging on the cross that led directly to his death is only one part of the suffering. Jesus' suffering all started just after he was arrested at the garden of Gethsemane while praying with his disciples when they were weary and sleepy. Roman soldiers took him to the home of the high priest where one of the soldiers, in a moment of sycophantic rage, slapped him. Jesus was then taken to Pilate, and after Pilate found no fault worthy of death, he tried (in his own way) to save Jesus by scourging him. In an effort to impress the Jews that Jesus had been severely and sufficiently beaten, bruised, battered, and punished, Pilate hoped this action would pacify them. But he did not reckon with the vicious anger and hatred (motivated by Satan) that they had for Jesus. If we look at John 19:1, it simply says, "Then Pilate took Jesus and scourged him." What did this simple statement mean? Perhaps the simplicity of the statement hid the wickedness and excruciating pain that was inflicted upon Jesus. In a way, this suffering may have been lost on many; however, it was a horrible thing.

The Roman scourge was an implement designed to inflict cruel and severe bodily punishment. It had a handle as well as (usually) twelve leather cords that had jagged pieces of bones and or metal attached in order to make each blow more painful and effective. A victim was tied to a post, stripped of clothing, (exposing the back and body) as the whip was applied with extreme force on the exposed back and skin. Each blow cut the skin open in several places at the same time because of the twelve branches (so to say). Assuming the scourge used on Jesus had twelve thongs then he would have received 468 stripes on his body for the 39 lashes, and according to Isaiah 52:14, his body was so marred (disfigured) that he was not recognized.

> As many were astonied at thee; his visage was so marred more than any man, and his form more than the sons of men.

Usually, the pain from scourging is so severe that the victim faints during the flogging. It was in this state that Pilate brought Jesus to the Jews saying, "Behold the man" (John 19:14), but what did they say? "Crucify him" (15). As we continue to read, we learn more about how the events unfolded.

> Then delivered he him therefore unto them to be crucified. And they took Jesus, and led him away. And he bearing his cross went forth into a place called the place of a skull, which is called in the Hebrew Golgotha: Where they crucified him, and two other with him, on either side one, and Jesus in the midst. (16–18)

What these simple statements convey to the reader of the Bible again hide the very wicked and painful form of death that crucifixion is. On the cross, Jesus was tortured, brutalized as his sinless blood was shed for the entire human race (past, present, and future). He was nailed to the cross as if they were nailing lifeless wood to wood. He suffered intense pain as his flesh and bones were both crushed and pierced by those huge nails. If you imagine the pain associated with piercing your finger with a very little pin, or by mistakenly jamming the door of your house or car against your fingers, and then compare it with what Jesus would have gone through as the nails were being pounded steadily through his body to the cross, it is difficult to even fathom his pain. And it didn't stop there! He was stripped naked for all to see, and then his body was nailed to cross. Can you imagine the excruciating pain Jesus must have experienced as the cross was being raised to stand upright with his body on it? The weight of his body was held in place by the nails. As he hung there on the cross, breathing became difficult, and as he began to suffocate, he had to push himself up using the base at his feet for support. He had to do this in order to get much needed oxygen into his lungs, even with his scourge-battered back against the cross' rough surface, which would lead to more pain.

Someone may point out that Jesus was not the only unjust victim of death by crucifixion and that others went through similarly excruciating pain and discomfort. This is true, however, we have given some of this graphic detail of the pain and suffering that led to Jesus' death on the cross because those sufferings and pain have a spiritual counterpart and life-changing implications for mankind. A number of things happened *pari-passu* (at the same time) that were in the realm of the spirit and were not seen with the naked human eyes as they occurred. The spiritual effects of this event have so much to offer the human race and we shall look at some of them as well as the specifics of what they offer to human beings who believe.

On the cross Jesus was bruised, wounded, and made to taste bitterness when he was offered wine, mixed with gall; but after tasting it, he refused to drink it (Matt 27:34 NIV). Why did Jesus refuse this drink? The drink was usually offered to those who were crucified or scourged because it contained some form of analgesic designed to reduce the intensity of pain. By refusing, Jesus submitted and subjected himself willingly to endure all the terrible pain and discomfort that we should have suffered for our sins and he became our pain bearer. He took away our pain.

> Surely he took up our pain and bore our suffering, yet
> we considered him punished by God, stricken by him,
> and afflicted. (Isa 53:4 NIV)

On the cross Jesus was hungry and thirsty but he did not accept drink until the end.

> After this, Jesus knowing that all things were now accomplished, that the scripture might be fulfilled, saith, I thirst. (John 19:28)

Each of the above scenarios is very significant. The sum total on the cross is that Jesus was destitute and in want of all things. This is a picture of horrible poverty in addition to the agonizing rejection he suffered on the cross. He was also rejected by men.

> He is despised and rejected of men; a man of sorrows, and acquainted with grief: and we hid as it were our faces from him; he was despised, and we esteemed him not. (Isa 53:3)

Not only was he rejected by men, he was again rejected by his father while on the cross.

> And about the ninth hour Jesus cried with a loud voice, saying, Eli, Eli, lama sabachthani? that is to say, My God, my God, why hast thou forsaken me? (Matt 27:46)

This is very powerful because both of them had been inseparable from eternity past.

> In the beginning was the Word, and the Word was with God, and the Word was God. The same was in the beginning with God. (John 1:1–2)

WHY GOD REJECTED JESUS

Jesus was rejected because God cannot behold sin. The Bible tells us in Habakkuk 1:13, "Thou art of purer eyes than to behold evil, and canst not look on iniquity." By virtue of Adam's sin in the garden of Eden, man is separated from God.

> Surely the arm of the LORD is not too short to save, nor his ear too dull to hear. But your iniquities have separated you from your God; your sins have hidden his face from you, so that he will not hear. (Isa 59:1-2 NIV)

Spiritually, Jesus carried our sins when he hung on the cross to die in our stead. This is not seen with physical human eyes but was recorded for us.

> All we like sheep have gone astray; we have turned every one to his own way; and the LORD has laid on him the iniquity of us all. (Isa 53:6)

> Who his own self bare our sins in his own body on the tree that we, being dead to sins, should live unto righteousness: by whose stripes ye were healed. (1 Pet 2:24)

Why was Jesus rejected? He was rejected because God cannot tolerate sin. And so on the cross, Jesus not only carried our sins, but in addition to that, God made him become sin for us as stated in 2 Corinthians 5:21.

> For he hath made him to be sin for us, who knew no sin; that we might be made the righteousness of God in him.

Sin and its consequences are at the root of all the problems that have ever confronted man, from Adam to date.

> Therefore, just as sin entered the world through one man, and death through sin, and in this way death came to all people, because all sinned. (Rom 5:12 NIV)

Given that disobedience to divine instructions and the consequences of such disobedience is at the root of most of the calamities befalling man, it is important to note that disobedience to instructions leads to death, both spiritual and physical. In the midst of a world riddled with sin and uncertainties, God in his wisdom and mercy proffers a solution that erases sin and death. A plan that will address this issue of sin permanently must be very significant to man and this is what Jesus did on the cross.

> But the gift is not like the trespass. For if the many died by the trespass of the one man, how much more did God's grace and the gift that came by the grace of the one man, Jesus Christ, overflow to the many! Nor can the gift of God be compared with the result of one man's sin: The judgment followed one sin and brought condemnation, but the gift followed many trespasses and brought justification. For if, by the trespass of the one man, death reigned through that one man, how much more will those who receive God's abundant provision of grace and of the gift of righteousness reign in life through the one man, Jesus Christ!
>
> Consequently, just as one trespass resulted in condemnation for all people, so also one righteous act resulted in justification and life for all people. For just as through the disobedience of the one man the many were made sinners, so also through the obedience of the one man the many will be made righteous.
>
> The law was brought in so that the trespass might increase. But where sin increased, grace increased all the more, so that, just as sin reigned in death, so also grace might reign through righteousness to bring eternal life through Jesus Christ our Lord. (Rom 5:15–21)

As we have earlier stated, we reiterate that the cross of Jesus Christ is the most important event in the history of the entire human race for all eternity. This is true because it is the venue where the demonstration of God's love, mercy, and grace took place.

> And as Moses lifted up the serpent in the wilderness, even so must the Son of man be lifted up: That whosoever believeth in him should not perish, but have everlasting life. For God so loved the world, that he gave his only begotten Son, that whosoever believeth in him should not perish, but have everlasting life. (John 3:14–16)

Further to that, the Bible declares that the greatest demonstration of love is to lay down one's life for their friends. For example, military personnel in any nation demonstrate great love for their nation. They hazard their lives for the protection of their nation. Christians are soldiers of Christ who should demonstrate brotherly love and tolerance regardless of race, color, gender, or economic or political differences that threaten the unity of the country today. All these differences ought to be laid aside for the good of all.

> Greater love hath no man than this that a man lay down his life for his friends. (John 15:13)
>
> Hereby perceive we the love [of God], because he laid down his life for us: and we ought to lay down [our] lives for the brethren. (1 John 3:16)
>
> See what great love the Father has lavished on us, that we should be called children of God! And that is what we are! The reason the world does not know us is that it did not know him. (3:1)

Where was this love lavished on us? We see it on the cross when Jesus Christ the Son of God laid down his life for us. God demonstrated his love for us in that while we were still sinners, Christ died for us. Recall that sin is at the root of all our troubles on earth. Therefore, when sin was taken away from us, all the evil consequences of sin were taken away from us as well, including death because sin brought death with it. These consequences can no longer bother us if we know who we are in him, stay away from sin, and enforce our rights and privileges as God's children.

THE POWER OF LOVE

There are many misconceptions about love out there in the world, and many people see love from their various backgrounds, upbringing, spirituality, religious beliefs, etc. Some equate love with feelings, hence, we hear people say, "I love you," and later say, "I don't love you anymore." There has to be more to love than all this. The *Macquarie Dictionary* defines love as "The benevolent affection of God for his creatures or the reverent affection due from them to God."[4]

The Bible gives us some concrete ideas of what love is in several passages of scripture. For example, let us look at declarations about love in both the *Amplified Bible* and *New Living Translation* of 1 Corinthians 13:4–8.

> Love endures long and is patient and kind; love is never envious nor boils over with jealousy, is not boastful or vainglorious, does not display itself haughtily. It is not conceited (arrogant and inflated with pride); it is not rude (unmannerly) and does not act unbecomingly. Love (God's love in us) does not insist on it's own rights or it's own way, for it is not self-seeking; it is not touchy or fretful or resentful; it takes no account of the evil done to it (it pays no attention to a suffered wrong). It does not rejoice at injustice and unrighteousness, but rejoices when right and truth prevail. Love bears up under anything and everything that comes, is ever ready to believe the best of every person, its hopes are fadeless under all circumstances, and it endures everything (without weakening). Love never fails (never fades out or becomes obsolete or comes to an end). (AMP)

> Love is patient and kind. Love is not jealous or boastful or proud or rude. It does not demand its own way. It is not irritable, and it keeps no record of being wronged. It does not rejoice about injustice but rejoices whenever

---

[4] *Macquarie Dictionary*, online ed., s.v. "love."

the truth wins out. Love never gives up, never loses faith, is always hopeful, and endures through every circumstance. Prophecy and speaking in unknown languages and special knowledge will become useless. But love will last forever! (NLT)

Note the last statement of the verse in the NLT: "But love will last forever!" This is far different from what many think and believe to be love. Many people think they can love today and hate tomorrow. For example, in marriage, couples often say they love each other. But a few years later, the same couple that stood before the altar of God and said, "I do," will turn their backs and say, "No, I don't." But they said they were in love! That's not the love of God. The love of God is true love. True love is love that lasts forever. The Bible says, "He that loveth not knoweth not God; for God is love" (1 John 4:8). Loving in this sense is loving with the God kind of love that is not sentimental, not ephemeral or transient. God is love and God is eternal, so love is eternal, i.e., love lasts forever. This statement means that, those who say they love today and later say they hate the fellow they say they once loved do not really know what true love is.

God is not just love, but everything he does is motivated out of pure love. This is why he did what he did for mankind when we did not even know about him. There are many who do not have any mental conception of this kind of love. I remember sharing the gospel message with someone of another faith and he just kept asking me why did God do that? "It does not make sense to me," he said. I tried to explain that God is infinitely love and all he does for his creatures is from the purest kind of love imaginable, but the young man kept saying, "I don't get it." Ephesians 3:19 shares with us how to gain this understanding: by believing in and accepting the love of Christ.

> And to know the Love of Christ which passeth knowledge, that ye might be filled with all the fullness of God.

The love of God is beyond what we can know with our mental

(thinking) faculties. That is probably why the young man could not understand why God did what he did for mankind—to send his son to die in our stead so that we could be saved. That is also why some people do not want to accept the gift offered, because they do not understand the reason and say it does not make sense to them that God should do what the Bible says he did for us. The Bible is filled with truth and so what it says is factual. What God did is what gives us the hope of eternal life we now have today. When someone offers me a good gift, I accept the gift first, and then thank the giver, before asking why they gave me the gift.

The cross of Christ is not just a message of love, but it is a love gift from a loving God who cares for us and loves us beyond what we can ever comprehend. All we need to do is accept the love gift that he offers. May you catch a revelation of that love, in Jesus' name, as you read this book. Ephesians 3:19 further says, "that ye might be filled with all the fullness of God." Is it not wonderful that in one of the verses the Bible says we can be filled with all the fullness of God? Receiving this fullness has to do with knowing the love of Christ. May you encounter and know this love as you read on in Jesus' name. If we can all love each other the way God loves us, what a fantastic place this world will be. Imagine a world void of violence, fraud, corruption, stealing, lying, cheating, etc., as we cannot do these things to each other anymore. Why? Because 2 Corinthians 5:14 says, "The love of Christ constraineth us." What a joy that would be! It is this love that moved God to make a way for him to punish the sin of mankind on his behalf in order to pardon man. This is what the cross of Jesus offers us: a message of forgiveness. On the cross, Jesus became the sacrifice for our sin so that we can obtain forgiveness. Therefore the cross has a message of forgiveness to all who believe in what Jesus did. Ephesians 1:7 assures us of redemption.

> In whom we have redemption through his blood, the forgiveness of sins.

Jesus shed his blood on the cross for the forgiveness of sins. Observe what this passage says and allow this truth to sink in: redemption and forgiveness of sins come through the blood of Jesus. No matter how steeped in sin or how far gone you may think you are, on the cross, Jesus through his sacrificial death, purchased your pardon and offers you forgiveness for all your sins—known and unknown. Some have said they don't know how God can ever forgive them for all the terrible things that they have done. If you or someone you know harbor such thoughts, the Bible clearly says,

> Come now, and let us reason together, saith the LORD: though your sins be as scarlet, they shall be as white as snow; though they be red like crimson, they shall be as wool. (Isa 1:18)

No matter how bad you think you are, the blood of Jesus will make you good again in the sight of Almighty God. The Bible says the blood will so wash you that you will be white as snow.

> But if we walk in the light, as he is in the light, we have fellowship one with another, and the blood of Jesus Christ his Son cleanseth us from all sin. (1 John 1:7)

The blood of Jesus not only washes clean, it gives a new beginning with God. God gives each one of us the opportunity to fulfill our destiny, and a very good example is Saul of Tarsus who is also known as Paul the Apostle. Paul was a man who persecuted the believers in Christ at the beginning stages of the church. He passionately and aggressively sought and arrested Christians and then suddenly converted to Christianity, changed his ways, and started aggressively to preach Christ as the crucified and risen Savior.

WHAT CAUSED PAUL TO CHANGE SO DRAMATICALLY?

Paul had a wrong belief based on his understanding of the Old Testament Torah. According to Deuteronomy 21:23, he believed that for Jesus to have died by hanging on a cross meant that he was accursed of God and so could not be the Messiah his followers claimed that he was. Paul was so incensed by this that he actually persecuted the church (believers in and followers of Jesus) and wanted to destroy it completely. He was on this mad mission when Jesus mercifully confronted him as stated in Acts 9:3-7:

> As he neared Damascus on his journey, suddenly a light from heaven flashed around him. He fell to the ground and heard a voice say to him, Saul, Saul, why do you persecute me? Who are you, Lord? Saul asked. I am Jesus, whom you are persecuting, he replied. Now get up and go into the city, and you will be told what you must do. The men traveling with Saul stood there speechless; they heard the sound but did not see anyone.

This encounter with the resurrected Jesus did so much to his psyche that it realigned his belief. He immediately concluded that for Jesus (who was crucified and buried) to be alive meant that he had risen from the dead.

But why is this so important? How can someone who sinned and was accursed by God (as Paul thought then), be raised from the dead by the same Holy God? Obviously, since God raised him from the dead, Jesus did not die for personal sin. So Paul concluded that Jesus must have died a sacrificial death for other people's sin, and God accepted his sacrifice and raised him back to life. God's actions really got Paul's attention and made him do a rethink, and so he started preaching and teaching that the same Jesus was the Son of God as well as the Messiah. Acts 9:20 tells us,

At once he began to preach in the synagogues that Jesus is the Son of God.

What convinced Paul? The resurrection of Jesus was so convincing it could not be denied. Paul later wrote in Romans 1:4 that Jesus was, "declared to be the Son of God with power, according to the spirit of holiness, by the resurrection from the dead." And now we can all rejoice, hallelujah, Jesus is alive and lives forevermore. So we see the power and effect that the resurrection of Jesus can have and has had over the years, starting from biblical times.

Jesus is the only person who lived on this planet earth to date who not only accurately predicted his own death, but also had the audacity to book an appointment post death and keep it. The disciples witnessed the prediction of his death and resurrection and their recollections are shared in several places in the Bible.

> When they had sung a hymn, they went out to the Mount of Olives. Then Jesus told them, "This very night you will all fall away on account of me, for it is written:
> "'I will strike the shepherd, and the sheep of the flock will be scattered.'
>
> But after I have risen, I will go ahead of you into Galilee." (Matt 26:30–32 NIV)
>
> "Don't be alarmed," he said. "You are looking for Jesus the Nazarene, who was crucified. He has risen! He is not here. See the place where they laid him. But go, tell his disciples and Peter, 'He is going ahead of you into Galilee. There you will see him, just as he told you.'" (Mark 16:6–7 NIV)

Pay attention to the words "as he told you." Jesus kept the appointment post death. And not only did Jesus keep this appointment, he then reassured the disciples and began to give them instructions for spreading the gospel message.

> Then Jesus said to them, "Do not be afraid. Go and tell my brothers to go to Galilee; there they will see me." (Matt 28:10 NIV)
>
> Then the eleven disciples went to Galilee, to the mountain where Jesus had told them to go. When they saw him, they worshiped him; but some doubted. Then Jesus came to them and said, "All authority in heaven and on earth has been given to me. Therefore go and make disciples of all nations, baptizing them in the name of the Father and of the Son and of the Holy

Spirit, and teaching them to obey everything I have commanded you. And surely I am with you always, to the very end of the age." (16–20)

Jesus had the audacity to book an appointment with his disciples ahead of his death (to meet them after his death), and now makes another bold declaration to those who believe, telling them he will be with them always. To those who doubt, I would say that if he kept the appointment with his disciples after his death, which he did, we should have the confidence to boldly declare that this promise of life after death will also be kept. Without Jesus' sacrificial death on the cross, there would not have been a resurrection. I pray for every reader of this book that the death on the cross and resurrection of Jesus Christ will have such powerful effects on you and in your life in Jesus' name.

Following the course of these events, Paul changed from persecuting the church, to charting a new beginning. He began preaching the gospel that he had fought against and wanted to stop from spreading, and he became the greatest apostle of the New Testament. Every action confirms what Jesus said to his disciples before he went to the cross.

> And I say also unto thee, That thou art Peter, and upon this rock I will build my church; and the gates of hell shall not prevail against it. (Matt 16:18)

As it was then that no force was able to stop the Church of Jesus Christ, so it still is today. Before his conversion to becoming a believer of Christ, when Paul, also known as Saul, was a chief persecutor of the budding church at that time, Jesus confronted him near Damascus.

> And as he journeyed, he came near Damascus: and suddenly there shined round about him a light from heaven: And he fell to the earth, and heard a voice saying unto him, Saul, Saul, why persecutest thou me? And he said, Who art thou, Lord? And the Lord said, I am Jesus whom thou persecutest: it is hard for thee to kick against the pricks. (Acts 9:3–5)

Again today, just as it happened to Paul, a known persecutor of the church, so it is happening to people in these modern days. Recently, on YouTube I saw stories of former Muslim terrorists who converted to Christianity after they had encounters (in their dreams according to their posted video statements) with Jesus Christ the resurrected Savior.

The love of Christ as shown on the cross still upholds the cross' message of forgiveness. To forgive means to grant a pardon for offense committed, to cancel an indebtedness. In the history of the human race, Adam, our progenitor before he birthed us, sinned against God, and lost the glory, consciousness, and presence of God. He then had the nature of sin with a death sentence hanging over him, and under this condition he gave birth to the human race. The result? We all inherited what he had; we were born in sin, born with a depraved nature of sin, and with a death sentence hanging over our heads.

> Therefore, just as sin entered the world through one man, and death through sin, and in this way death came to all men, because all sinned—for before the law was given, sin was in the world. But sin is not taken into account when there is no law. Nevertheless, death reigned from the time of Adam to the time of Moses, even over those who did not sin by breaking a command, as did Adam, who was a pattern of the one to come. (Rom 5:12–14 NIV)

The result of this nature of sin that we were born with is that we rebelled against God by going our own ways.

The laying of our iniquity on Jesus is what made our forgiveness possible in order that the integrity of God's Word be maintained. Sin began with Adam in the garden of Eden. Several passages in the book of Romans address the issue of sin.

> For all have sinned and come short of the Glory of God. (3:23)

For the wages of sin is death; but the gift of God is eternal life through Jesus Christ our Lord. (6:23)

In the words of Pastor E. A. Adeboye of The Redeemed Christian Church of God, death is the salary sin attracts. This death was hanging over every human being but was taken away on our behalf by Jesus Christ through his sacrificial death on the cross. Romans 6:23 goes on to say, "but the gift of God is eternal life through Jesus Christ our Lord." Everyone who works is entitled to their salary, therefore salary is a must, a right, an entitlement, and a must have, but a gift is not compulsory, it can be accepted or rejected, and therefore the one being offered a gift has a right to accept or reject the gift.

This gift of eternal life is on offer from God and is available to every human being regardless of their faith, belief or nonbelief, background, race, upbringing, etc. This gift is available to every human being through Jesus Christ alone, and let me repeat for emphasis, it is available to every human being on the face of this planet without exception and only through Jesus Christ alone. Remember what the scripture says,

For God loved the world so much that he gave his one and only Son, so that everyone who believes in him will not perish but have eternal life. (John 3:16 NLT)

Observe that scripture said God loved the world, meaning that God's love is all-inclusive, that no one is excluded. Anyone that does not accept this free gift is responsible for excluding themselves. They are in effect saying that they are ready to pay the debt hanging over them that Jesus took away on the cross. Note that when God forgives anyone who accepts the sacrifice that Jesus made for our sins on the cross, he forgives so completely that there is no record of it against that person. In addition, the person is given a new beginning with him no matter how terrible the person was previously. Paul, (again) is a classic example. He once persecuted the church, but Jesus and the Father did not hold it against him. He was actually chosen to carry the name of Jesus to the gentiles. Can you beat that for forgiveness?

Ours is a living example of how gracious our God can be. I was not only forgiven, but also called to preach the gospel to every creature; to share a personal encounter I had with the Lord. This happened on the last Tuesday morning of September 1994. On September 27, at about five minutes before 7:00 a.m., while worshiping the Lord alone and unaware of whether I was asleep or awake, I heard a loud voice that came from behind me. The voice said, "Go into all the world and preach the gospel." I immediately turned around to see who spoke, only to realize that I was alone, all by myself at home. Immediately, joy that I could not explain flooded my heart. You see, before that morning, as a young bachelor, I had determined to know the Lord, draw close to him, and serve him. Each time we gathered in the church during testimony times, fellow believers would get up to testify, in the course of which they made statements like … the Lord spoke to me, God told me this, God told me that, etc. After awhile this began to drive me to seek the Lord more and desire to hear his voice even if only once. I cried to him saying, "Lord, if it is only one time, just speak to me, let me know what your voice sounds like. Let me know I belong to you." At some point, thoughts flashed through my mind, like I did not really belong to the Lord, and that the Lord had really not forgiven me for all the sins I had committed. These thoughts really bothered me as a young Christian. So, you can imagine how I felt when I realized that the Lord just spoke to me. I stood up at our next prayer vigil on Friday, September 30, 1994, to testify that I heard the Lord speak to me.

> Keep on asking, and you will receive what you ask for. Keep on seeking, and you will find. Keep on knocking, and the door will be opened to you. For everyone who asks, receives. Everyone who seeks, finds. And to everyone who knocks, the door will be opened. You parents—if your children ask for a loaf of bread, do you give them a stone instead? Or if they ask for a fish, do you give them a snake? Of course not! So if you sinful people know how to give good gifts to your children, how much more will your heavenly Father give good gifts to those who ask him. (Matt 7:7–11 NLT)

Those who search will surely find me. (Prov 8:17 NLT)

THE GIFT OF HOPE

Hope is an expectation of positive outcome. It is an attitude of the mind. It keeps one optimistic. We, those who put our trust and faith in Christ and what he did on the cross, receive that eternal life only through faith in what Jesus did on the cross. "For God so loved the world, that he gave his only begotten Son, that whosoever believeth in him should not perish, but have everlasting life" (John 3:16). Because of that, we know that when we die, there is a far more glorious future awaiting us in his presence.

> But as it is written, Eye hath not seen, nor ear heard, neither have entered into the heart of man, the things which God hath prepared for them that love him. (1 Cor 2:9)

We know that there are mansions awaiting our arrival in heaven, so we have hope that one day, we shall inhabit those mansions.

> Let not your heart be troubled: ye believe in God, believe also in me.
>
> In my Father's house are many mansions: if it were not so, I would have told you. I go to prepare a place for you. And if I go and prepare a place for you, I will come again, and receive you unto myself; that where I am, there ye may be also. (John 14:1–3)
>
> If in this life only we have hope in Christ, we are of all men most miserable. (1 Cor 15:19)

This passage clearly states that it is not only in this life that we have hope. We have hope of eternal life and so even at the point of death we have hope and should not sorrow as others who have no hope do.

> But I would not have you to be ignorant, brethren, concerning them which are asleep, that ye sorrow not, even as others which have no hope. (1 Thess 4:13)

At the time of death, sorrow is for those who do not have hope. Let us affirm this by reading in 1 Peter.

> Blessed be the God and Father of our Lord Jesus Christ, which according to his abundant mercy hath begotten us again unto a lively hope by the resurrection of Jesus Christ from the dead. (1:3)

> Wherefore gird up the loins of your mind, be sober, and hope to the end for the grace that is to be brought unto you at the revelation of Jesus Christ. (13)

We have hope because there is something glorious ahead of us that we shall receive when Jesus returns for his saints. This hope is made possible through the sacrifice of Jesus on the cross. The cross gives us hope of life after death and living successfully in this world. This hope demonstrates God's love and compassion for humanity, and totally defeats death and sin for our sake. All of this points us to the fact that the cross of Christ is of tremendous significance for man.

Chapter 3

WHAT IS THE SIGNIFICANCE OF THE CROSS?

There are at least two events, so far, that have shaped the history of the human race in her relationship with God, and both of them were separations resulting from sin. But fortunately for mankind, God found a way for us to overcome sin through the life, death, and resurrection of his son, Jesus Christ.

The first of the two events of separation took place in the garden of Eden, after man sinned when he rebelled against God's express instruction not to eat the fruit on the tree in the midst of the garden.

> And the LORD God commanded the man, saying, Of every tree of the garden thou mayest freely eat: But of the tree of the knowledge of good and evil, thou shalt not eat of it: for in the day that thou eatest thereof thou shalt surely die. (Gen 2:16–17)

Later, as Adam and Eve walk through the garden of Eden and defy God's command, they experience the reality of their actions. Their disobedience has led to the introduction of sin into the world.

> When the woman saw that the fruit of the tree was good for food and pleasing to the eye, and also desirable for gaining wisdom, she took some and ate it. She also gave some to her husband, who was with her, and he ate it. Then the eyes of both of them were opened, and

> they realized they were naked; so they sewed fig leaves together and made coverings for themselves. Then the man and his wife heard the sound of the LORD God as he was walking in the garden in the cool of the day, and they hid from the LORD God among the trees of the garden. But the LORD God called to the man, "Where are you?" He answered, "I heard you in the garden, and I was afraid because I was naked; so I hid." (Gen 3:6–10 NIV)

They ran away from the presence of the Lord rather than run to him because they had sinned and were afraid. Adam said he heard God's voice in the garden and was afraid. Sin brings fear. There was no fear in their relationship until sin entered, and then suddenly they ran from the presence of God. To this day, sin (still) drives people away from the presence of God, or better still, the devil uses the feeling of guilt as a result of committed sin to make people run away from the Lord's presence.

The second major event of separation, which is the greatest event in humanity, is the separation that took place on the cross, when Jesus took the sin of the entire human race upon himself. There, the Father rejected him. Rejection can be very painful to the one that is rejected. On the cross, Jesus felt the pain of his father's rejection so severely that we notice it in the way he cried out.

> And about the ninth hour Jesus cried with a loud voice, saying, Eli, Eli, lama sabachthani? that is to say, My God, my God, why hast thou forsaken me? (Matt 27:46)

But why was Jesus rejected? Remember that sin had become a barrier between God and man from the moment Adam sinned in the garden. Once sin was introduced into the world man could not approach God. Jesus was rejected so that you and I could now be accepted back to the Father. This is a spiritual benefit or result of the sacrifice Jesus made on the cross. On the cross, God put our sin on Jesus; Jesus carried our sin and took the punishment so that we can receive forgiveness. In 2

Corinthians 5:21 the Bible says, "For he hath made him to be sin for us, who knew no sin; that we might be made the righteousness of God in him." The moment God placed our sin on Jesus while he hung on the cross the following things happened: God (life) was separated from Jesus, Jesus was therefore rejected, and the separation of life from him and the pain of rejection led to his physical death.

On the cross, Jesus took the place of the entire human race and died a substitutionary death to pay the price for our sin, the original sin of rebellion against God that was at the base of every other sin man has committed. The cross of Christ is the place of the death of Jesus Christ, the place where he died to save the entire human race.

> When Jesus therefore had received the vinegar, he said, It is finished: and he bowed his head, and gave up the ghost. (John 19:30)

THE MIRACLES ON THE CROSS

The cross creates room for the miracle of our reconciliation with God, while Jesus dying on the cross opens up communication again between God and man.

a. *The cross is the place where our sins were removed.* Sin is the major barrier to our relating with God. Hence, there is need for it to be removed from our path to communing with God and that is exactly what the cross has done. Jesus fulfilled the requirement.

> Who his own self bare our sins in his own body on the tree that we, being dead to sins, should live unto righteousness: by whose stripes ye were healed. (1 Pet 2:24)

> Blotting out the handwriting of ordinances that was against us, which was contrary to us, and took it out of the way, nailing it to his cross. (Col 2:14)

He was manifested to take away our sins. (1 John 3:5)

b. *The cross is the place of forgiveness.* There is no need for us to die in our sins and self-guilt because forgiveness is made available to all through the cross.

> And you, being dead in your sins and the uncircumcision of your flesh, hath he quickened together with him, having forgiven you all trespasses. (Col 2:13)

> We have redemption through his blood, the forgiveness of sins, according to the riches of his grace. (Eph 1:7)

c. *The cross is the place where enmity was removed.* The cross eliminated the animosity, the hostility and enmity between God and man that was created when sin entered the world. Access to God was made impossible because of the enmity, but it was restored through the cross. The cross created access to the Father through salvation (new birth) and the name of Jesus Christ the Son.

> Having abolished in his flesh the enmity, even the law of commandments contained in ordinances; for to make in himself of twain one new man, so making peace. (Eph 2:15)

d. *The cross is the place of redemption.* There is redeeming grace that we can access through the blood of Jesus that was shed on the cross.

> Who hath delivered us from the power of darkness, and hath translated us into the kingdom of his dear Son: In whom we have redemption through his blood, even the forgiveness of sins. (Col 1:13–14)

e. *The cross is the place of reconciliation.* Reconciliation was possible only after enmity was removed by Jesus' death on the cross.

> And that he might reconcile both unto God in one body by the cross, having slain the enmity thereby. (Eph 2:16)
>
> Now all things are of God, who has reconciled us to Himself through Jesus Christ, and has given us the ministry of reconciliation, that is, that God was in Christ reconciling the world to Himself, not imputing their trespasses to them, and has committed to us the word of reconciliation. (2 Cor 5:18–19 NKJV)

f. *The cross is the place of adoption.* God decided in advance to adopt us into his own family by bringing us to himself through Jesus Christ. This is what he wanted to do, and it gave him great pleasure.

> Having predestinated us unto the adoption of children by Jesus Christ to himself, according to the good pleasure of his will. (Eph 1:5)
>
> Now therefore ye are no more strangers and foreigners, but fellow citizens with the saints, and of the household of God. (Eph 2:19 NLT)

g. *The cross is the place where access to the Father was established.* On the cross God's rejection of man was removed so that man could now have access to his creator and Father.

> I am the way, the truth, and the life: no man cometh unto the Father, but by me. (John 14:6)
>
> For through him we both have access by one Spirit unto the Father. (Eph 2:18)

h. *The cross is the place of blessing.* The cross is the place of blessing because it changed God's disposition toward human beings as the enmity between God and us was removed. God now looks on us in his favor and not his wrath. To me, this is probably the greatest gift.

> Blessed be the God and Father of our Lord Jesus Christ, who hath blessed us with all spiritual blessings in heavenly places in Christ. (Eph 1:3)
>
> Because one person disobeyed God, many became sinners. But because one other person obeyed God, many will be made righteous. (Rom 5:19 NLT)

i. *The cross is the place where the issue of sin was settled forever.* On the cross, God visited all his righteous anger on sin to the point of rejecting his own son because in obedience to God, his Son carried our sin on himself. Do not forget that sin is at the root of most, if not all, our troubles. These consequences can no longer affect us if we know who we are in him and if we stay away from sin and enforce our rights and privileges as God's children.

God's holiness demands that he deal with sin wherever it rears its head. Sin separates us. As sin was removed from us, all the evil consequences of sin were removed, including sickness, poverty, curses, failure, shame, rejection, demonic oppression (pressed down in your sleep at night), sexual violation while sleeping (wet dreams), spirit spouse, sexual perversion like bestiality and homosexuality (many may disagree with this), frequent miscarriage or abortion, and all forms of addiction, such as pornography, tobacco, alcohol, sex, and drugs.

> Wherefore, as by one man sin entered into the world, and death by sin; and so death passed upon all men, for that all have sinned. (Rom 5:12)
>
> But this man, because he continueth ever, hath an unchangeable priesthood. Wherefore he is able also to save them to the uttermost that come unto God by him, seeing he ever liveth to make intercession for them. (Heb 7:24–25)

j. *The cross is the place where the spirits behind addictions and demonic oppression were totally disarmed.* The spirits lost their power or hold over the entire human race. They are no longer permitted to trouble those who believe in Jesus anymore, except when people open the door for those spirits to come back again through sin. For example, when an accused man is found not guilty, all chains with which they had him bound are removed and he is given his freedom and full rights. So it is with us in the kingdom of God. We are no longer guilty before God. All our rights and privileges have been restored through the sacrifice on the cross. The enforcers have been disarmed and can no longer force us to do anything against our will. We are totally free. Hallelujah!

> He canceled the record of the charges against us and took it away by nailing it to the cross. In this way, he disarmed the spiritual rulers and authorities. He shamed them publicly by his victory over them on the cross. (Col 2:14–15 NLT)

k. *The cross is the place where all the evil consequences of our sins were taken away.* Jesus died on the cross not only to take away our sins, but also to take away the evil consequences of our sins. One of those consequences was curse.

The only way to take away our curse was to become a curse on our behalf and the only way to do so was to die on the cross himself on our behalf because the Bible says anyone that is hung on the tree is accursed of God. So, Jesus had to die by hanging in order to become accursed of God so that God may heap our curses on him and release us from those curses. Just as he had to receive stripes on his body in order for us to be healed; so also he had to hang on a tree (cross) so as to take away our curses. This is the message of the cross: that on the cross, God demonstrated his love for us when he (in Christ Jesus) took away our sin with all the consequences that sin carries. He reconciled us to himself through the blood that Jesus shed while also disarming the enemy that had enforced the consequences of sin.

> Christ hath redeemed us from the curse of the law, being made a curse for us: for it is written, cursed is every one that hangeth on a tree. (Gal 3:3)

If a man has committed a sin worthy of death and he is put to death, and you hang him on a tree, his corpse shall not hang all night on the tree, but you shall surely bury him on the same day (for he who is hanged is accursed of God), so that you do not defile your land which the LORD your God gives you as an inheritance. (Deut 21:22–23)

HOW TO GAIN ACCESS TO THE THRONE OF GRACE

Through the cross God created an avenue for man to regain the access to him that was lost when Adam sinned at the garden of Eden in the beginning of man's history. This sin separated man from God and this separation, a.k.a. enmity, was removed by Jesus on the cross. Before the sacrifice of Jesus on the cross, man could not access the presence of God. During the days of the Old Testament, the high priest alone could approach the holy of holies and he could only access this sacred place once a year, after completing some very serious preparations.

> Now when these things were thus ordained, the priests went always into the first tabernacle, accomplishing the service of God. But into the second went the high priest alone once every year, not without blood, which he offered for himself, and for the errors of the people: The Holy Ghost this signifying, that the way into the holiest of all was not yet made manifest, while as the first tabernacle was yet standing. (Heb 9:6–8)

At this point in history the way to access God had not yet been manifested. Man was denied access to God until the cross. Today every believer in Christ has direct access into the very presence of the living God.

To put it in context, lest its significance be lost on us, we realize that ordinarily most citizens do not have access to their government leaders and political office holders, even though they go to great lengths to try to get politicians to hear their views and concerns. They write letters, make phone calls, and expend lots of time, energy, and money to gain the attention of political leaders who can affect change. Yet all people, including politicians, athletes, movie stars, and the like, were created and are alive today because God deemed it so. They don't have any more privilege regarding life and death than anyone else. The Bible declares that God can take their lives from them without any possibility of protest and no one can challenge him for doing so.

> Now see that I, *even* I, *am* He, And *there is* no God besides Me; I kill and I make alive; I wound and I heal; Nor *is there any* who can deliver from My hand. (Deut 32:39 NKJV)

> And at the end of the time I, Nebuchadnezzar, lifted my eyes to heaven, and my understanding returned to me; and I blessed the Most High and praised and honored Him who lives forever: For His dominion *is* an everlasting dominion, And His kingdom *is* from generation to generation. All the inhabitants of the earth *are* reputed as nothing; He does according to His will in the army of heaven And *among* the inhabitants of the earth. No one can restrain His hand Or say to Him, "What have You done?" (Dan 4:34–35 NKJV)

These words in Daniel chapter 4 are from the lips of King Nebuchadnezzar, who was addressed as a king of kings, here acknowledging the greatness of the God of heaven and earth after God humbled him for seven years and then restored him back as king. Note the last statement where he said (concerning God) no one can restrain God's hand or question what he has done. This is the God who can raise anyone out of nowhere and make them king.

> The LORD kills and makes alive; He brings down to the grave and brings up. The LORD makes poor and makes

> rich; He brings low and lifts up. He raises the poor from the dust *And* lifts the beggar from the ash heap, To set *them* among princes And make them inherit the throne of glory. "For the pillars of the earth *are* the LORD's, And He has set the world upon them." (1 Sam 2:6–8 NKJV)
>
> For promotion cometh neither from the east, nor from the west, nor from the south. But God is the judge: he putteth down one, and setteth up another. (Ps 75:6–7)

This Almighty God can help anyone who belongs to him through what Jesus did on his cross. We (who believe) have direct unimpeded access to God without going through a third party, minister, mentor, or personal assistant. We don't have to have an elevated status in the world, nor do we have to spend lots of money to have access to God. He is available to all. We can lead a life of true privilege, a life that is not based on temporal things, when we choose to use our access to the One who matters most.

The cross of Christ is our access key card to the throne of grace where we obtain forgiveness of sin and experience the power thereof. Access is the ability, right, or permission to approach, enter, speak, or use. On the cross, through his sacrifice, Jesus created this access to God for all who will believe. Every born again child of God therefore has the permission, right, and ability to approach the Holy God at any time of the day or night without any possibility of being denied access into God's presence. All we need to do is say Father, in the name of Jesus, and we are right in God's presence—just like that. This ability is powerful and needs to be meditated upon because access is very important in our daily lives here on earth.

In some of the more civilized societies throughout the world, people are regarded based on the access they have to authority. It is such that, those who did not want to have anything to do with you yesterday, suddenly begin to fuss over you the moment they realize that you have access to the seat of government or power. All of a sudden high society personalities want you to attend their events because they know you have access to the corridors of power. But in John 14:6, the Bible tells us,

> Jesus saith, I am the way, the truth, and the life: no man cometh unto the Father, but by me.

Every (genuinely converted) Christian has express access into the immediate presence of God without booking an appointment or passing through security checks or waiting at a reception area.

HOW TO INFLUENCE POLITICAL LEADERS

Access to the throne of grace is very important because it may be a fact that we do not have access to authority figures in our land, yet we have access to the one who controls all political leaders. Through prayers in the name of Jesus, we can actually get whatever we desire from those political leaders that we cannot access.

> The king's heart is in the hand of the LORD, as the rivers of water: he turneth it whithersoever he will. (Prov 21:1)

If the body of Christ can properly understand and utilize this access, the will of God will be done on earth as it is in heaven. When this access is properly deployed, Christians will determine what happens wherever they find themselves, no matter how few they are. This is because while the political leader may be at the official government office governing, the Christians, through access to God in prayer, can actually be the ones who determine what happens. How is this so? We go to God because he is the one who controls each leader's heart and thoughts. We can pray for things to happen in the way that it will bless the body of Christ and God's kingdom.

Let me share a true-life experience. It was in the year 2008, and there was a state of apprehension and uncertainty in the city of Port Harcourt, Nigeria, due to kidnapping and the general state of insecurity. About this time, motorbikes were commonly used as a means of unorganized public transportation with all sorts of stories told about how criminals and kidnappers used motorbikes to commit their acts. A local assembly of the body of Christ at the Redeemed Christian Church of God (RCCG) Amazing Grace Parish G.R.A Phase 2 extension in Port Harcourt, where

I pastored at that time, gathered together and prayed to God asking that the government ban the use of motorbikes as acceptable means of public transportation on our streets. Guess what? On the December 31, 2008, the governor banned motorbikes from the streets of Port Harcourt and that ban still stands today. Glory be to God! We had no access to the governor, neither did we go to see him, nor protest on the streets. But we got him to do what we desired to see happen in our city through our access to the Father, in the name of God the son, Jesus Christ.

The heart of every leader is in the hands of God because he turns it whichever way it pleases him. Through God the father, believers can influence decisions made by political leaders.

> Just as water is turned into irrigation ditches, so the Lord directs the king's thoughts. He turns them wherever he wants to. (Prov 21:1 TLB)

Another good example of how believers in our congregation properly deployed and obtained desired results happened when we gathered to hold night vigils to pray over the state of affairs in the Niger Delta region of Nigeria. At this point in time, some parts of Rivers and Bayelsa states were really dangerous places in which to live and move about due to atrocities being committed by groups of individuals that were described as Niger Delta militants.

During those vigils, we prayed to God the Father for an end to the militancy and for peace to return to our states and to our communities. We took authority over the wicked spirits that were behind this militancy by commanding them in the name of Jesus to stop all their activities that were disturbing our peace in the Niger Delta region. Glory to God, government created an enabling environment for the militants to turn in their arms, and therefore militancy came to an end. A large number of confirmed militants surrendered to government forces, were disarmed, and then rehabilitated. Some were even sent to learn and acquire new skills outside of Nigeria, such as in South Africa.

Do we claim absolute responsibility for an end to militancy in the Niger Delta region? No. A number of activities may have contributed, however, we believe that our prayers played some role that made it possible for the federal government to create the environment that made the militants willing to surrender their arms and openly embrace peace. Hallelujah to Jesus for access to the Father who can control even militants' hearts.

Access to the most powerful personality in the universe makes us almost as powerful through our prayers. One man, Daniel, altered the course of the history of his nation (see Daniel 9). Elijah singlehandedly caused famine for three and a half years when he prayed that God should withhold rain, and it happened exactly as he desired from God.

> Elijah was as human as we are, and yet when he prayed earnestly that no rain would fall, none fell for three and a half years! Then, when he prayed again, the sky sent down rain and the earth began to yield its crops. (Jas 5:17–18 NLT)

This is a man who operated under the Old Testament. Think of how much more we of the New Testament (who have the name of Jesus and access to the Father in that name) can do with this access. The cross of Christ gives us access to spiritual power.

Chapter 4

WHAT IS THE MESSAGE OF THE CROSS?

The *Merriam-Webster Dictionary* defines "message" in the following three ways: a communication conveyed in writing, in speech, or by signals; a messenger's errand or function; and an underlying theme or idea.[5] The definitions that are most appropriate in this case are one and three. Thus we can say that message is the underlying theme of any event, of information, news, advice, etc. The message can be conveyed through writing or proclamation. To proclaim means to preach. The underlying theme of the crucifixion of Christ can be conveyed by writing or by preaching. The preacher must preach the information that the cross communicates. Therefore, the message of the cross is the information the cross communicates.

The cross of Christ has assumed a very important place in world history because events since the death of Christ have been measured by the distance that separate them from it. The cross signifies the instrument of crucifixion; and hence crucifixion itself, namely, that of Christ. The crucifixion is loaded with various messages, but when we talk about the cross, what exactly does it convey to us? Our main text on this subject is 1 Corinthians 1:17–18 (NIV), specifically looking at verse 18.

> For the message of the cross is foolishness to those who are perishing, but to us who are being saved it is the Power of God.

---

[5] *Merriam-Webster Dictionary*, 2017 online ed., s.v. "message."

This passage tells us that the cross contains at least two things: message and power. This implies that when people hear the Gospel message (how Jesus Christ suffered and died on the cross for mankind and rose from the dead after three days), some will believe and accept it while others mock and or reject it. To those who accept, it is the power of God, because they experience the power of God to turn a sinner into a saint. However, our focus in this chapter is on the message of the cross while a later chapter looks at the power of the cross of Christ.

HOW THE CROSS CAN CHANGE LIVES

What is the message that the cross conveys to those who have come to put their trust in Christ, and how can this message change peoples' lives? Here are some of the messages that the cross of Jesus Christ communicates to those who hear about it, but they are definitely not all.

a. *The cross has a message of redemption.* Redemption is available for all mankind through the death (and the blood that was shed) on the cross by Jesus. He died on the cross to save (redeem) mankind. Redemption means deliverance or freedom from sin, to rescue, or to pay off. Ephesians 1:7 says,

> In whom we have redemption through his blood, even the forgiveness of sins, according to the riches of his grace. (KJV)

> He is so rich in kindness and grace that he purchased our freedom with the blood of his Son and forgave our sins. (NLT)

This message says there is redemption for every human being who puts his or her faith (or trust) in what Jesus did for mankind on the cross. Anyone who believes that Jesus died for them on the cross and rose again the third day, and confesses Jesus as their Lord, shall be saved.

> Neither is there salvation in any other: for there is none other name under heaven given among men, whereby we must be saved. (Acts 4:12)
>
> If thou shalt confess with thy mouth the Lord Jesus, and shalt believe in thine heart that God hath raised Him from the dead, thou shalt be saved. (Rom 10:9)

b. *The cross has a message of love for all human beings on the face of this planet.* Every human being deserves to be loved and desires to be loved. God has given us examples to demonstrate unfailing love.

> For God so loved the world that he gave his only begotten Son, that whosoever believeth in him should not perish, but have everlasting life. (John 3:16)
>
> There is no greater love than to lay down one's life for one's friends. (John 15:13 NLT)
>
> We know what real love is because Jesus gave up his life for us. So we also ought to give up our lives for our brothers and sisters. (1 John 3:16 NLT)
>
> God showed this great love for us by sending Christ to die for us while we were still sinners. (Rom 5:8 NLT)

The cross of Christ not only conveys a message of love but it is a love gift from a loving God who cares for us and loves us beyond what we can ever comprehend. All we need to do is accept the love gift that he offers. May you catch a revelation of that love as you read this book in Jesus' name.

c. *The cross has a message of forgiveness.* We looked at Ephesians earlier in this section as it pertained to redemption, and now we see that redemption and forgiveness go hand in hand. Redemption involves the payment of debt owed. A debt cancelled by the creditor is forgiven of the debtor. Christ paid our debts that we might be forgiven.

> In whom we have redemption through his blood, the forgiveness of sins, according to the riches of his grace. (Eph 1:7)

It was on the cross that his blood was shed for the forgiveness of our sins. No matter how steeped in sin or how far you may think you have gone; on the cross, Jesus, through his sacrificial death, purchased your pardon and offers you forgiveness from all your sins known and unknown.

> Come now, and let us reason together, saith the LORD: though your sins be as scarlet, they shall be as white as snow; though they be red like crimson, they shall be as wool. (Isa 1:18)

> But if we walk in the light, as he is in the light, we have fellowship one with another, and the blood of Jesus Christ his Son cleanseth us from all sin. (1 John 1:7)

The cross is saying to everyone that there is forgiveness of sin from God for whoever will put their trust in and accept the sacrifice that Jesus made on the cross. To forgive means to grant pardon for offense committed, to cancel indebtedness. God cancelled our indebtedness on the cross.

In the history of mankind, Adam, our progenitor, sinned against God, lost the glory and presence of God, took on the nature (body of sin) with a death sentence hanging on him when he birthed us. So we are all born in sin, with the nature of sin and the indebtedness hanging over our heads. Scripture says,

> All we like sheep have gone astray; we have turned everyone to his own way; and the LORD hath laid on him the iniquity of us all. (Isa 53:6)

Note the last statement. God laid our iniquity on Jesus so that he could punish our sin (through Jesus) in order for us to be pardoned while maintaining the integrity of God's word and his holiness.

d. *The cross has a message of hope.* Jesus is the hope of eternal life, which God, who cannot lie, promised before the world began (Titus 1:2) and being justified by his grace, we should be made heirs according to the hope of eternal life (3:7). Every believer in Christ has hope of eternal life and hopes that one day, they will see Jesus. Through the cross, everyone who believes and receives Jesus as Lord has been offered eternal life.

> Behold, what manner of love the Father hath bestowed upon us, that we should be called the sons of God: therefore the world knoweth us not, because it knew him not. Beloved, now are we the sons of God, and it doth not yet appear what we shall be: but we know that, when he shall appear, we shall be like him; for we shall see him as he is. And every man that hath this hope in him purifieth himself, even as he is pure. (1 John 3:1–3)

> The wicked is driven away in his wickedness: but the righteous hath hope in his death. We have hope even in death. (Prov 14:32)

> Dear brothers and sisters, we want you to know what will happen to the believers who have died so you will not grieve like people who have no hope. For since we believe that Jesus died and was raised to life again, we also believe that when Jesus returns, God will bring back with him the believers who have died. We tell you this directly from the Lord: We who are still living when the Lord returns will not meet him ahead of those who have died. For the Lord himself will come down from heaven with a commanding shout, with the voice of the archangel, and with the trumpet call of God. First, the Christians who

have died will rise from their graves. Then, together with them, we who are still alive and remain on the earth will be caught up in the clouds to meet the Lord in the air. Then we will be with the Lord forever. So encourage each other with these words. (1 Thess 4:13–18 NLT)

There is hope for us even in death. I love the way verse 13 puts it: "we don't want you to be uninformed about those who sleep in death so that you do not grieve like the rest of mankind who have no hope." We have hope even in death. Death is not the end for us; we have hope of eternal life, hope of being with Jesus. We have hope.

e. *The cross has a message of blessings.* God desires the best for his children. He has blessed them with everything that pertains to life and godliness in order to make their lives worth living.

> Blessed be the God and Father of our Lord Jesus Christ, who hath blessed us with all spiritual blessings in Heavenly places in Christ. (Eph 1:3)

Observe that the passage says "all." What does all mean? All means the "whole of something." This implies that nothing was left out. The passage says that God hath blessed us with all spiritual blessings. These blessings were, and still are, made available to us through what Jesus did on the cross.

f. *The cross has a message of healing.* Healing is a major part of what Jesus did while he was here on earth in the flesh because sickness is one of the major consequences introduced by sin and the devil.

> How God anointed Jesus of Nazareth with the Holy Ghost and with power: who went about doing good, and healing all that were oppressed of the devil; for God was with him. (Acts 10:38)

This passage tells us how Jesus went about doing good, and it also gives us an idea of what sickness is: an oppression of the devil. Sin is a burden extremely heavy for man to carry. Anything that burdens man is oppressive. Sin is a burden to the human soul. Sickness is a burden to the human body. There are many physical illnesses, for example if we exert too much stress on our body and fail to rest, our body will likely suffer a breakdown of some sort and we may become sick or even hospitalized. If we do not mind what we eat and take in a lot of junk food, there will be consequences such as obesity, high blood pressure, diabetes, etc. One important thing to note here is that when such conditions occur, usually the sickness responds to medication and treatment. However, there are some illnesses that are unresponsive to medication and treatment. Such physical conditions usually have spiritual undertones.

How do we identify illnesses that are just mere physical sickness from those that have spiritual causes? As stated earlier, a mere physical illness will usually respond to medication and resolve within the prescribed period of recovery from that particular illness. Sicknesses that have spiritual origin or those caused by activities of demons or agents of darkness are usually untreatable. These illnesses hide in the body and therefore are unlikely to be seen physically no matter which diagnostic tests are used, and they are usually longstanding conditions. Two examples of physical ailments that had spiritual causes are seen in the story of the woman who had an issue with her blood (see Mark 5:25–34) and that of the bound daughter of Abraham (see Luke 13:11–18). Both cases are considered under *The cross has a message of deliverance* in the next section.

Healing is not only a major part of what Jesus did while he walked the streets of Galilee, Capernaum, and Jerusalem, it is also an important part of what happened on the cross. Each human being is entitled to it when they receive Jesus as Lord.

> The thief cometh not, but for to steal, and to kill, and to destroy: I am come that they might have life and that they might have it more abundantly. (John 10:10)

Sickness is one of the works of the devil that Jesus came to destroy.

> But, he that committeth sin is of the devil; for the devil sinneth from the beginning. For this purpose the Son

of God was manifested, that he might destroy the works of the devil. (1 John 3:8)

HOW JESUS DESTROYED THE WORKS OF THE DEVIL

According to the Bible, Jesus destroyed the works of the devil through the anointing.

> How God anointed Jesus of Nazareth with the Holy Ghost and with power: who went about doing good, and healing all that were oppressed of the devil; for God was with him. (Acts 10:38)

Isaiah saw this about the ministry of Jesus and said something interesting and revealing.

> But he was wounded for our transgressions, he was bruised for our iniquities: the chastisement of our peace was upon him; and with his stripes we are healed. (Isa 53:5)

Isaiah, from the Old Testament, foresaw what Jesus was going to do on the cross. He looked forward to it, while Peter, from the New Testament, quoted the passage as a living witness who was there when it happened. He was now looking back to what happened on the cross when he said,

> Who his own self bare our sins in his own body on the tree that we, being dead to sins, should live unto righteousness: by whose stripes ye were healed. (1 Pet 2:24)

Note that Peter used past tense when he said, "by his stripes we were healed," not that we are going to be healed but that we were already healed. Our healing was settled on the cross of Christ. Healing was made available to us through what happened to Jesus on the cross.

Also note that Peter talked about our healing in the same place where he talked about Jesus carrying away our sins on his body on the cross.

The lesson here is that the issue of sin has to be dealt with for the healing virtue to flow freely from the body of Jesus to all of mankind. The message the cross conveys is that there is healing available to mankind through the finished work of Christ on the cross. There is healing for us through the stripes that broke the body of Jesus on the cross. Note that everywhere Jesus went people were healed, whether he touched them, as in Matthew 8:1-3, or they touched him, as in Mark 5:25-34. In either case the result was the same: people were healed.

In addition to healing, Mark 16:17-18 says that believers are given even more authority.

> These signs shall follow them that believe; In my name shall they cast out devils; they shall speak with new tongues; They shall take up serpents; and if they drink any deadly thing, it shall not hurt them; they shall lay hands on the sick, and they shall recover.

From this scripture, Jesus has given believers the right and authority to use his name to lay hands on the sick and heal them. When believers lay hands on the sick and say, in the name of Jesus, a demand is placed on agents of the kingdom of darkness responsible for the sickness to remove their hands of oppression from that sick person. A demand is also placed on Jesus to ensure that the sick fellow received their healing for the glory of Jesus' name. John 14:14 clearly states, "If ye shall ask any thing in my name, I will do it." Bible scholars say that a more accurate translation of that verse should be, "If ye shall demand anything in my name, even if it does not exist, I will create it." So go ahead and demand in Jesus' name.

The cross of Christ delivers four messages and the only thing we need to do to activate them is to believe in them.

a. *The cross has a message of deliverance.* The devil's grip is strong, but Jesus' power is even stronger.

> Giving thanks unto the Father, which hath made us meet to be partakers of the inheritance of the saints in light: Who hath delivered us from the power of darkness and hath translated us into the kingdom of his Son. (Col 1:12–13)

Deliverance means being set free from oppression or from bondage. Before Jesus came, we were all slaves to sin and the devil. That is why Jesus answered,

> Verily, verily, I say unto you, Whosoever committeth sin is the servant of sin. (John 8:34)

> Know ye not, that to whom ye yield yourselves servants to obey, his servants ye are to whom ye obey; whether of sin unto death, or of obedience unto righteousness? But God be thanked, that ye were the servants of sin, but ye have obeyed from the heart that form of doctrine which was delivered you. Being then made free from sin, ye became the servants of righteousness. I speak after the manner of men because of the infirmity of your flesh: for as ye have yielded your members servants to uncleanness and to iniquity unto iniquity; even so now yield your members servants to righteousness unto holiness. For when ye were the servants of sin, ye were free from righteousness. What fruit had ye then in those things whereof ye are now ashamed? for the end of those things is death. But now being made free from sin, and become servants to God, ye have your fruit unto holiness, and the end everlasting life. (Rom 6:16–22)

All human beings beginning with the first man, Adam, who committed sin, have sin nature in them. It is this nature of sin that makes everyone sin whether they want to or not. Moreover, the nature of sin from Adam brought separation from God and resulted in slavery to sin and the devil. Furthermore, through sin, the door opened for the devil and evil spirits to gain access where they could then afflict victims.

> He that diggeth a pit shall fall into it; and whoso breaketh an hedge, a serpent shall bite him. (Eccl 10:8)

There are many people who are under various kinds of bondage and are struggling against forces too powerful for them (including suicidal tendencies) to overcome. To compound the problem, these forces that they battle against are unseen, yet they are present and sometimes compel people to do things against their will.

The Bible tells the story of a young boy whose father came to Jesus asking for help for his son who was afflicted with an evil spirit.

> And one of the multitude answered and said, Master, I have brought unto thee my son, which hath a dumb spirit; And wheresoever he taketh him, he teareth him: and he foameth, and gnasheth with his teeth, and pineth away: and I spake to thy disciples that they should cast him out; and they could not. He answereth him, and saith, O faithless generation, how long shall I be with you? how long shall I suffer you? bring him unto me. And they brought him unto him: and when he saw him, straightway the spirit tare him; and he fell on the ground, and wallowed foaming. And he asked his father, How long is it ago since this came unto him? And he said, Of a child. And oftentimes it hath cast him into the fire, and into the waters, to destroy him: but if thou canst do anything, have compassion on us, and help us. Jesus said unto him, If thou canst believe, all things are possible to him that believeth. And straightway the father of the child cried out, and said with tears, Lord, I believe; help thou mine unbelief. When Jesus saw that the people came running together, he rebuked the foul spirit, saying unto him, Thou dumb and deaf spirit, I charge thee, come out of him, and enter no more into

him. And the spirit cried, and rent him sore, and came out of him: and he was as one dead; insomuch that many said, He is dead. But Jesus took him by the hand, and lifted him up; and he arose. (Mark 9:17–27)

Note that evil (unseen) spirits were behind the boy's physical (seen) affliction, and the boy was helpless against those evil forces that tried to force him to jump into fire or water in order to destroy him. But when Jesus cast out the evil spirits, they left him.

Addiction is a form of bondage because it is the state of being enslaved to a habit or practice or to something that is psychologically or physically habit-forming. Many are addicted to different vices, such as drugs, alcohol, pornography, prostitution, or sexual perversions such as lesbianism, homosexuality, or bestiality. Some people do not like the substance or behavior they are addicted to and actually desire to be free, but find themselves powerless against the forces behind these vices. The reason for their seeming inability to resist the forces is because the forces are unseen evil spirits that compel them against their will. Just like the boy in the passage was powerless against the forces that compelled him to such tendencies, so too people struggle against evil forces today. Whatever it is that compels you to do anything against your will is from the devil and his fellow agents of darkness, not of God, as God never forces anyone against their will. These agents of darkness (unseen evil spirits) are the forces behind all forms of addiction and perversion.

No matter what you or anyone you know may be addicted to, that addiction is controlled by these forces of darkness, and the good news message is that on the cross Jesus defeated (disarmed) all the forces of darkness put together and in the process delivered all of mankind from every power of darkness and their vice-like grip over us. If you are struggling with any form of addiction, and you repent of your sins, accept and confess Jesus as Lord and Savior, deliverance from those evil powers is yours instantly because they were already disarmed on the cross.

> When you were dead in your sins and in the uncircumcision of your flesh, God made you alive with

> Christ. He forgave us all our sins, having canceled the charge of our legal indebtedness, which stood against us and condemned us; he has taken it away, nailing it to the cross. And having disarmed the powers and authorities, he made a public spectacle of them, triumphing over them by the cross. (Col 2:13–15)

Jesus triumphed over them through the cross. This means that for every believer, the forces of darkness are powerless because they have been disarmed. They have nothing to attack you with anymore if you know your right and enforce it.

From the Bible, we discover that sometimes people suffer physical ailments that are a result of unseen evil spirit activities. Jesus dealt with two of these that will serve as illustrations. The first story is in Luke 13:11–16, where a woman was bound by satanic forces that manifested a physical condition that could be described as Kyphosis. Kyphosis is a permanent curving of the spine that makes somebody look hunched over and it is often attributed to arthritis. However, in the case of the woman, her physical ailment did not respond to medical treatment, the anointing was required to destroy the yoke of the devil holding her down in a hunched position for eighteen years.

> And, behold, there was a woman which had a spirit of infirmity eighteen years, and was bowed together, and could in no wise lift up herself. And when Jesus saw her, he called her to him, and said unto her, Woman, thou art loosed from thine infirmity. And he laid his hands on her: and immediately she was made straight, and glorified God. And the ruler of the synagogue answered with indignation, because that Jesus had healed on the sabbath day, and said unto the people, There are six days in which men ought to work: in them therefore come and be healed, and not on the sabbath day. The Lord then answered him, and said, Thou hypocrite, doth not each one of you on the sabbath loose his ox or his ass from the stall, and lead him away to watering? And

> ought not this woman, being a daughter of Abraham, whom Satan hath bound, lo, these eighteen years, be loosed from this bond on the sabbath day?

The second story, found in Mark 5:25-34, is that of the woman whose name was swallowed by her ailment and became known as the woman with the issue of blood. In this case, what looked so routine lasted twelve years, exhausted all her savings, and yet she remained ill until she made contact with the anointing that was on Jesus.

> And a certain woman, which had an issue of blood twelve years, And had suffered many things of many physicians, and had spent all that she had, and was nothing bettered, but rather grew worse, When she had heard of Jesus, came in the press behind, and touched his garment. For she said, If I may touch but his clothes, I shall be whole. And straightway the fountain of her blood was dried up; and she felt in her body that she was healed of that plague. And Jesus, immediately knowing in himself that virtue had gone out of him, turned him about in the press, and said, Who touched my clothes? And his disciples said unto him, Thou seest the multitude thronging thee, and sayest thou, Who touched me? And he looked round about to see her that had done this thing. But the woman fearing and trembling, knowing what was done in her, came and fell down before him, and told him all the truth. And he said unto her, Daughter, thy faith hath made thee whole; go in peace, and be whole of thy plague.

When the woman came to touch Jesus' clothes, hers was not an ordinary touch; it was a touch loaded with the faith to receive. The Bible says faith comes by hearing. When she heard about Jesus, she pressed in to touch, believing that if she could just touch his clothes she would be healed. This confession gave her the faith to receive and verse 28 tells us that when she touched him, she received.

These two stories show us some profound truths. When physical conditions are longstanding and have not responded to medical treatment, the cause is often evil spirits that must be dealt with before the victim can be healed. Again the good news of the Gospel message is that Jesus dealt with all evil satanic forces and defeated them openly on the cross.

Anyone who makes Jesus their Lord through the open confession of their mouths, has been delivered from the powers of darkness and come under his protection and power. Those agents of darkness lost the legal rights and the power to torment or violate believers because Jesus disarmed them on the cross.

b. *The cross of Jesus Christ has a message of victory.* Every human being desires to be victorious in life. Jesus has given us triumphant victory over the power of darkness.

> And having spoiled principalities and powers, he made a shew of them openly, triumphing over them in it. Let no man therefore judge you in meat, or in drink, or in respect of an holyday, or of the new moon, or of the sabbath *days.* (Col 2:15–16)

On the cross, Jesus disarmed powers and authorities that the kingdom of darkness arrayed against us, and gave us the victory. He gave us victory without a fight, victory without sweat.

> For everyone born of God overcomes the world. This is the victory that has overcome the world, even our faith. (1 John 5:4 NIV)

The cross has a message of victory for everyone and it is based on what Jesus did. We need only to enforce the victory that had been won for us. And this is easy because the enemy has been disarmed by our commander in chief, Jesus Christ. Hallelujah!

> But thanks be to God! He gives us the victory through our Lord Jesus Christ. (1 Cor 15:57 NIV)

Victory means to subdue, conquer, overcome, and prevail. In life, there are many unseen battles that we fight; however, in this case we already have the victory, which means that we enter the battle from the position of strength. The enemy's weapons have been taken away by Jesus on the cross, his only remaining weapon is fear. So the devil tries to use symptoms and thoughts against us to put fear in our minds. But if we remember that Jesus has already disarmed the devil, it follows that the devil or his agents cannot hurt or harm us. Fear loses its power over us and we can use the word of God to counter the attack from the devil through the thoughts he plants in our minds. For every attack of the devil through thoughts that bring fear, we can counter such attacks with scripture.

> For though we walk in the flesh, we do not war according to the flesh. For the weapons of our warfare *are* not carnal but mighty in God for pulling down strongholds, casting down arguments and every high thing that exalts itself against the knowledge of God, bringing every thought into captivity to the obedience of Christ. (2 Cor 10:3–5 NKJV)

This shows that the battle is really in the mental realm and we use scripture to defeat the devil in the mental realm. For example, when the devil sows thoughts that you cannot do this or that, because of one symptom of sickness or the other, we counter the thought using scripture such as Philippians 4:13 that says, "I can do all things through Christ which strengthens me." Friend, remember that even before we showed up, we already had victory over the devil through Jesus and what he did on the cross. Romans 8:37 says that we are not just victorious, but we are more than conquerors through him that loved us.

Jesus is the one who loves us and washed us from our sins in his blood.

> And from Jesus Christ, who is the faithful witness, the firstborn from the dead, and the ruler of the kings of the earth. (Rev 1:5)

To him who loves us and has freed us from our sins by his blood be all the glory forevermore. Hallelujah, praise Jesus! Note that though the battle is in the mind (mental realm), the only weapon through which we can defeat the devil is the word of God. This is exactly what Jesus our Lord and perfect example did when he was confronted by the devil. See Matthew 4:1–10, where on each occasion, Jesus responded to the devil's temptation by quoting scripture. Here we quote verse 4 (KJV):

> But he answered and said, It is written, Man shall not live by bread alone, but by every word that proceedeth out of the mouth of God.

It is written then he quoted from Deuteronomy 8:3 (NKJV):

> Man shall not live by bread alone; but man lives by every word that proceeds from the mouth of the LORD.

This is the pattern for everyone who desires to live a victorious Christian life after accepting and confessing Jesus as Lord and Savior. We must take the scripture and let it dwell inside of us through confessing the word of God and meditating on scripture. As we do so, Jesus and his word will abide in us and Jesus will become more real to us. Hence, John 15:5 and 7 say we should abide in him and let his words abide in us. As we speak the word, meditate, and obey it in totality, the word of God comes to abide in us in this way. When we give ourselves wholly to the word it is then that we can enjoy the benefits and blessings of the victory of the cross of Jesus Christ.

c. *The cross has a message of peace.* The world all over is in search for peace. However, the world can only give relative peace. The ultimate tranquility that every human being desires is found in God.

> Therefore being justified by faith, we have peace with God through our Lord Jesus Christ. (Rom 5:1)

Peace with God can only come by faith in what Jesus did on the cross and it comes by him. Before Christ came, we were enemies of God. Isaiah 48:22 and 57:21 tell us,

> There is no peace, saith my God, to the wicked.

Peace is withheld from a certain category of people called the wicked. Who are the wicked and what does wicked mean in the Bible? The word wicked is from the Hebrew word *rasa*, which translates as wicked, evil, guilty, ungodly, condemned, and him that did wrong. In the eyes of God, all the world including human beings that are away from Jesus Christ lie in wickedness.

> And we know that we are of God, and the whole world lieth in wickedness. (1 John 5:19)
>
> But the transgressors shall be destroyed together: the end of the wicked shall be cut off. (Ps 37:38)
>
> The wicked shall be turned into hell, *And* all the nations that forget God. (Ps 9:17)

From scripture, we see that the Bible regards the wicked and those who keep God out of their lives as the same and both have a common destiny, hell. Hell is the place where all were destined to go before Jesus came to die in our stead and go there on our behalf so that we are spared that fate. The wicked are those outside the will of God. What is the will of God for mankind?

> Who desires all men to be saved and to come to the knowledge of the truth. (1 Tim 2:4)

The will of God is for all men to be saved. Men get saved when they believe and accept that the death, burial, and resurrection of Jesus was for them, and then they receive salvation by confessing Jesus as Lord and Savior.

> These things I have spoken unto you, that in me ye might have peace. In the world ye shall have tribulation: but be of good cheer; I have overcome the world. (John 16:33)

In Christ alone do we have real peace. Why is it that many are running here and there seeking peace but have not found it? They have been searching for peace in all the wrong places. If you are in that category, return to Jesus today and let his blood that was shed on the cross wash away your sin. The Father will reconcile you with himself as well as restore peace to your soul. This is when you will know true peace. And no matter the storms raging against you, you will be at peace, first within, and then it will radiate outwards and be seen by others. There are many people who are going through serious issues that will stretch the average person to the point of (some may describe as) driving them nuts, yet they are so cool, calm, and collected. Those around them even wonder how they cope in such an unruffled manner. The answer is that they have the peace that is found only in Christ, which passes all human understanding. Paul said in Philippians 4:6–7,

> Be careful for nothing; but in every thing by prayer and supplication with thanksgiving let your requests be made known unto God. And the peace of God, which passeth all understanding, shall keep your hearts and minds through Christ Jesus. (KJV)

> Then you will experience God's peace, which exceeds anything we can understand. His peace will guard your hearts and minds as you live in Christ Jesus. (NLT)

This is the great secret of our peace, as we "live in Christ Jesus." Hallelujah, praise Jesus! Remember also that peace is a fruit of the Spirit, as we read in Galatians 5:22:

> But the fruit of the Spirit is love, joy, peace, long suffering, gentleness, goodness, faith. (NIV)

> But the Holy Spirit produces this kind of fruit in our lives: love, joy, peace, patience, kindness, goodness, faithfulness. (NLT)

For those of us who are born again and filled with the spirit of Christ, our lives bear fruit, and peace is one element of the fruit of the

Spirit that is produced in us. Because it is a fruit of the Spirit, it follows that this kind of peace is not of the mind or mental realm; it does not depend on earthly circumstances or possessions. This is why one can be poor and have peace that even the rich do not have or know.

One of the ways the devil steals our peace is through thoughts of worry. We worry about things, worry about our children, about situations, about circumstances, etc. The purpose of worry is the same as the storm we see when Peter walks on water towards Jesus. As long as his eyes were on Jesus, he walked on water, but as soon as the storm increased, he shifted his eyes from Jesus and he began to sink. The story is in Matthew 14:25-32 (NIV).

> During the fourth watch of the night Jesus went out to them, walking on the lake. When the disciples saw him walking on the lake, they were terrified. "It's a ghost," they said, and cried out in fear. But Jesus immediately said to them: "Take courage! It is I. Don't be afraid." "Lord, if it's you," Peter replied, "tell me to come to you on the water." "Come," he said. Then Peter got down out of the boat, walked on the water and came toward Jesus. But when he saw the wind, he was afraid and, beginning to sink, cried out, "Lord, save me!" Immediately Jesus reached out his hand and caught him. "You of little faith," he said, "why did you doubt?" And when they climbed into the boat, the wind died down. Then those who were in the boat worshiped him, saying, "Truly you are the Son of God."

Peter actually walked on water based solely on the word Jesus said to him, "Come." When we step out in obedience to the word, we too can do the impossible. As long as Peter focused on Jesus, he walked on water but when he focused on the storm, he began to sink. When we stay on the word that Jesus gives us, the miraculous is possible. When we shift our focus from the word he gave and look at the circumstances surrounding us, we begin to sink. Circumstances may be a fact, they may be real, but the word Jesus gives us is truth. Truth does not change, while circumstances do change. Keep confessing the truth in the face of contrary circumstances and the circumstances will change and align with the truth. The word of God is truth (John 17:17).

It may be true that you or someone you know has been diagnosed with cancer, diabetes, hypertension, HIV, etc., but the truth is that on the cross, Jesus took these ailments away, and by his stripes, you have been healed. When we stay focused and maintain that confession in the face of contrary evidence, as you maintain the confession of faith and word, eventually, you will receive your healing. Halleluiah!

Observe that the moment Jesus and Peter got into the boat, the storm ceased. How come? I believe the main purpose of the storm in this passage was to take Peter's eyes and focus away from Jesus so that he could lose faith and sink. Once the lesson was learned and they stepped back into the boat, the storm ceased because it was no longer necessary.

The same thing happens in our day-to-day living, storms arise with the sole aim of removing our focus from the Lord Jesus Christ, knowing that in the Lord alone is our salvation, help, deliverance, etc. We need to remember to keep our eyes and minds on the Lord Jesus Christ so that we can experience his peace. Note that we keep our eyes and focus on Jesus through reading the Bible and meditating on its word.

d. *The cross brings us a message of access to the most important personality in the universe.* The most important personality on the whole planet, both in time and eternity, is God. Because of Jesus' death on the cross, we have access to the one who decides all that happens on earth, both now and in the future world, without end. We have access to the only one who not only can kill, but also can destroy souls in hell. We have access to the one who can show mercy to thousands of generations of those who love him and keep his commandments. We have access to the one who has no equal and is also called the Most High God. We have access to the one who opens a door that no one can shut and who can shut a door that no one can open. Revelation 3:7 describes this personality as,

> He that is holy, He that is true, He that hath the key of David, He that openeth, and no man shutteth; and shutteth, and no man openeth.

Before Jesus died on the cross, God's presence was inside the holy of holies, behind the veil, above the mercy seat, in between the two cherubim.

> And there I will meet with thee, and I will commune with thee from above the mercy seat, from between the two cherubims which are upon the ark of the testimony, of all things which I will give thee in commandment unto the children of Israel. (Exod 25:22)

No human being could enter this holy of holies except the high priest. And he could only do so once a year with great preparations and sacrifices.

> Now when these things were thus ordained, the priests went always into the first tabernacle, accomplishing the service of God.
>
> But into the second went the high priest alone once every year, not without blood, which he offered for himself, and for the errors of the people: The Holy Ghost this signifying, that the way into the holiest of all was not yet made manifest, while as the first tabernacle was yet standing. (Heb 9:6–8)

The reason for this state of things was the issue of sin that separated man from God right from the garden of Eden. Genesis 3:8 sheds more light on this.

> And they heard the voice of the LORD God walking in the garden in the cool of the day: and Adam and his wife hid themselves from the presence of the LORD God amongst the trees of the garden.

Sin brought enmity between man and the Holy God who cannot tolerate or behold sin. This state of enmity and separation between God and man continued from generation to generation; however, on the cross, by carrying our sin on his body, Jesus not only removed our sin from us but also carried it away from us. By doing this, he removed the enmity that was between us and God, and in the process made access to God possible, fulfilling what he said in John 14:6 (NLT), "I am the way, the truth, and the life. No one can come to the Father except through me."

When Jesus hung on the cross he cried out twice. Observe that at the moment Jesus carried our sins on the cross, God the father cut him off. This led to his cry in Matthew 27:46 (NIV): "About three in the afternoon Jesus cried out in a loud voice, *'Eli, Eli, lema sabachthani?'* (which means 'My God, my God, why have you forsaken me?')." The second time he cried out and then died, Jesus' purpose on earth was finished. His death allowed mankind direct access to God.

> And when Jesus had cried out again in a loud voice, he gave up his spirit. At that moment the curtain of the temple was torn in two from top to bottom. (Matt 27:50–51 NIV)

The curtain of the temple that tore in two from top to bottom in the scripture above reveals several things.

> The Holy Spirit was showing by this that the way into the Most Holy Place had not yet been disclosed as long as the first tabernacle was still functioning. This is an illustration for the present time, indicating that the gifts and sacrifices being offered were not able to clear the conscience of the worshiper. They are only a matter of food and drink and various ceremonial washings—external regulations applying until the time of the new order. But when Christ came as high priest of the good things that are now already here, he went through the greater and more perfect tabernacle that is not made with human hands, that is to say, is not a part of this creation. He did not enter by means of the blood of goats and calves; but he entered the Most Holy Place

once for all by his own blood, thus obtaining eternal redemption. (Heb 9:8–12 NIV)

Only blood can atone for sin. Without the shedding of blood there is no remission of sin. In the Old Testament, God allowed the blood of animals to atone for sin, but this was not adequate in the case of human beings. Verse 9 declares that the gift and the sacrifices could not clear the conscience of the worshipper. The blood of Jesus brought eternal redemption because it was more than qualified to pacify the wrath of God against sin.

Chapter 5

WHAT IS THE POWER OF THE CROSS?

Power is defined simply as the ability to do work. It is the ability to do or act, the capability of doing or accomplishing something. Jesus did many mighty miracles and works while he was on earth in the flesh. He opened blind eyes, including the eyes of those who were born blind. He cast out devils from many, including the one popularly called the mad man at Gadara (see Mark 5:1–16). He raised the dead several times, including Lazarus who was dead for four days and his body was already stinking, according to his sister. He fed 5,000 people with five loaves of bread and two fishes. He commanded the storm to seize. Everywhere he went people were astonished by the mighty miracles he performed. Yet, Jesus promised in John 14:12 that we will do greater works than those mighty works he did.

> Verily, verily, I say unto you, He that believeth on me, the works that I do shall he do also; and greater works than these shall he do; because I go unto my Father.

Jesus made this promise before he went to the cross where he stood in for us, and defeated the devil who held us in bondage (until that time) making us powerless against him (Satan) and his agents. How did Jesus do those works?

> How God anointed Jesus of Nazareth with the Holy Ghost and with power: who went about doing good, and

healing all that were oppressed of the devil; for God was with him. (Acts 10:38)

The anointing is the manifestation of the power of God. The Holy Ghost is the one through whom we receive the anointing. Wherever the Holy Ghost is, the anointing is present. See the statement Jesus made in Luke 4:18:

> The Spirit of the Lord is upon me, because he hath anointed me to preach the gospel to the poor; he hath sent me to heal the brokenhearted, to preach deliverance to the captives, and recovering of sight to the blind, to set at liberty them that are bruised.

Jesus went to the cross as our substitute and removed from us the thing that prevented us from having the Holy Ghost (the carrier and source of the anointing) dwell inside us. So now we can receive the Holy Ghost and have him reside inside us. Before he left the earth to go back to heaven, Jesus said some very interesting things about the power God makes available to us.

> And, behold, I send the promise of my Father upon you: but tarry ye in the city of Jerusalem, until ye be endued with power from on high. (Luke 24:49)

> But ye shall receive power, after that the Holy Ghost is come upon you: and ye shall be witnesses unto me both in Jerusalem, and in all Judaea, and in Samaria, and unto the uttermost part of the earth. (Acts 1:8)

Again note that the power comes only after the Holy Ghost has come upon us. Without the Holy Ghost there is no anointing or power. Jesus did not start ministry until he received the Holy Ghost.

On the day of Pentecost, the Holy Ghost, who helped Jesus while here on earth to do all the miracles and works that he did, came as promised. And we are told that this promise is also for us today.

> And when the day of Pentecost was fully come, they were all with one accord in one place. And suddenly there came a sound from heaven as of a rushing mighty wind, and it filled all the house where they were sitting. And there appeared unto them cloven tongues like as of fire, and it sat upon each of them. And they were all filled with the Holy Ghost, and began to speak with other tongues, as the Spirit gave them utterance. (Acts 2:1–4)

> Then Peter said unto them, Repent, and be baptized every one of you in the name of Jesus Christ for the remission of sins, and ye shall receive the gift of the Holy Ghost. For the promise is unto you, and to your children, and to all that are afar off, even as many as the Lord our God shall call. (38–39)

Observe that Peter who now preached before large gatherings of people on different occasions where three thousand and five thousand souls respectively were converted to Christianity, is the same Peter who cowardly denied Jesus three times in one night before his crucifixion.

> And with many other words did he [Peter] testify and exhort, saying, Save yourselves from this untoward generation. Then they that gladly received his word were baptized: and the same day there were added *unto them* about three thousand souls. (40–41)

> And as they spake unto the people . . . many of them which heard the word believed; and the number of the men was about five thousand. (4:1, 4)

> Simon Peter and another disciple were following Jesus. Because this disciple was known to the high priest, he went with Jesus into the high priest's courtyard, but Peter had to wait outside at the door. The other disciple, who was known to the high priest, came back, spoke to

> the girl on duty there and brought Peter in. "You are not one of his disciples, are you?" the girl at the door asked Peter. He replied, "I am not." It was cold, and the servants and officials stood around a fire they had made to keep warm. Peter also was standing with them, warming himself. . . . As Simon Peter stood warming himself, he was asked, "You are not one of his disciples, are you?" He denied it, saying, "I am not." One of the high priest's servants, a relative of the man whose ear Peter had cut off, challenged him, "Didn't I see you with him in the olive grove?" Again Peter denied it, and at that moment a rooster began to crow. (John 18:15-18, 25-27 NIV)

The Holy Ghost is what made the difference in Peter's life. Since that day of Pentecost, believers who have received the baptism in the Holy Spirit are empowered to demonstrate the power of the cross and also enabled by the Spirit to minister this baptism to other believers through, for example, the laying on of hands. Examples are found in Acts 8:14–17.

> Now when the apostles which were at Jerusalem heard that Samaria had received the word of God, they sent unto them Peter and John: Who, when they were come down, prayed for them, that they might receive the Holy Ghost: (For as yet he was fallen upon none of them: only they were baptized in the name of the Lord Jesus.) Then laid they their hands on them, and they received the Holy Ghost.

When Peter and John got to Samaria, they prayed for the new converts that they might receive, then laid hands on them to receive and they received the baptism of the Holy Ghost with evidence of speaking with new tongues. Other examples of where believers ministered the baptism in the Holy Ghost to other believers can be found in Acts 9:16–20 and 19:1–6.

Dear reader, this promise is also for you if you believe in Jesus and you have received as well as confessed him as your Lord and Savior according to Romans 10:9: "That if thou shalt confess with thy mouth the Lord Jesus, and shalt believe in thine heart that God hath raised him from the dead, thou shalt be saved." However, the question then is, how do I demonstrate the power of the cross of Christ?

HOW TO WIN THE FIGHT AGAINST SIN

According to the scriptures, Jesus came to destroy the works of the devil. First John 3:9 says, "He that committeth sin is of the devil; for the devil sinneth from the beginning. For this purpose the Son of God was manifested, that he might destroy the works of the devil." Destroying the works of the devil involved restoring life abundantly to man. Hence, John 10:10 says,

> The thief cometh not, but for to steal, and to kill, and to destroy: I am come that they might have life, and that they might have it more abundantly.

Whatever does not allow you to enjoy life fully is not of God and you can put an end to these activities in the name of Jesus as we shall see shortly.

The devil does his destructive work through the power of sin because sin drives away the presence of God, which leaves the field open for the devil to carry out those destructive activities. We see this the first time in the garden of Eden.

> They heard the voice of the LORD God walking in the garden in the cool of the day: and Adam and his wife hid themselves from the presence of the LORD God amongst the trees of the garden. (Gen 3:8)

> Son of man, seest thou what they do? even the great abominations that the house of Israel committeth here, that I should go far off from my sanctuary? but turn thee yet again, and thou shalt see greater abominations. (Ezek 8:6)

And Isaiah 59:1-2 puts it this way,

> Behold, the LORD's hand is not shortened, that it cannot save; neither his ear heavy, that it cannot hear: But your iniquities have separated between you and your God, and your sins have hid his face from you, that he will not hear.

Because of his holiness (holiness means total separation from sin) God cannot be anywhere there is sin, otherwise, he would have to judge it, and the result could be devastating.

Jesus came to restore what the devil stole including the loss of fellowship with our Heavenly Father and all the blessings and blessedness that go with that fellowship. On the cross, Jesus took away our sins by paying the penalty in full. Because of his total obedience and what he did on the cross, God the Father gave him a name above all other names.

> He [Jesus] humbled himself, and became obedient unto death, even the death of the cross. Wherefore God also hath highly exalted him, and given him a name which is above every name: That at the name of Jesus every knee should bow, of things in heaven, and things in earth, and things under the earth; And that every tongue should confess that Jesus Christ is Lord, to the glory of God the Father. (Phil 2:8-11)

From the above passage, we can see that it was because of what Jesus did on the cross that earned him this name from the Father. This name is above every name that we can ever think of and at the mention of the name Jesus every knee bows whether in heaven, on earth, or under the earth. They not only bow but they also confess that Jesus Christ is Lord to the glory of God the Father. Philippians 2:10-11 is a very real and profound truth that we can only experience as it happens in the invisible realm of the spirit, otherwise it could be lost to us. In other words, the power of the cross is demonstrable through the name of Jesus, and the authority the name carries in heaven, on earth, and underneath the earth.

Furthermore, we must understand that there are two dimensions to what happened on the cross: The physical (seen) realm as well as the spiritual (unseen) realm. In the physical realm, we see that Jesus suffered, was tortured, and then killed (crucified) when he was nailed to the cross. While these happened in the physical realm, things also happened in the spiritual realm and this spiritual aspect plays a very crucial role in both our relationship with God and the devil, and the hosts of hell.

HOW THE SPIRITUAL REALM CONTROLS THE PHYSICAL REALM

There is one very important point to note and remember always: The spiritual rules the natural or physical. Therefore, usually what we see play out in the natural world is a result of what has happened in the spiritual realm. And also, usually, concerning things divine, there is a spiritual, unseen aspect of what is seen in the natural physical world. One of the best examples of this can be found in the story of Job.

> One day the angels came to present themselves before the LORD, and Satan also came with them. The LORD said to Satan, "Where have you come from?" Satan answered the LORD, "From roaming throughout the earth, going back and forth on it." Then the LORD said to Satan, "Have you considered my servant Job? There is no one on earth like him; he is blameless and upright, a man who fears God and shuns evil." "Does Job fear God for nothing?" Satan replied. "Have you not put a hedge around him and his household and everything he has? You have blessed the work of his hands, so that his flocks and herds are spread throughout the land. But now stretch out your hand and strike everything he has, and he will surely curse you to your face." The LORD said to Satan, "Very well, then, everything he has is in your power, but on the man himself do not lay a finger." Then Satan went out from the presence of the LORD. (Job 1:6–12 NIV)

What followed this conversation was a calamity that befell Job in which he lost everything he had, on the same day, including his children, oxen and sheep, and servants. This means, many calamities that befall people today is a consequence of spiritual conversation as it happened in the case of Job. Then Job

> fell to the ground in worship and said: "Naked I came from my mother's womb, and naked I will depart. The LORD gave and the LORD has taken away; may the name of the LORD be praised." In all this, Job did not sin by charging God with wrongdoing. (20–22 NIV)

A close look at this passage reveals that before any of the calamities happened to Job in the natural, a conversation took place in the spiritual that had a direct bearing on Job.

In the case of our Lord Jesus Christ, if I were to ask someone, when was Jesus crucified? They would likely say the day he died physically on the cross. But if you ask God the Father, it happened even before the world was created, according to Revelation 13:8.

> All inhabitants of the earth will worship the beast—all whose names have not been written in the Lamb's book of life, the Lamb who was slain from the creation of the world.

Jesus was called the Lamb that was slain from the creation of the world.

If I may use the example of a simple anointing process to explain, we observe that physically what transpires is that we pour anointing oil on the person to be anointed, but it is what happens in the spiritual unseen realm that makes the anointing process anything at all. As the oil is applied physically, in the spirit realm the presence of God, in the person of the Holy Spirit, comes upon the person from that minute on. It is this aspect of the Spirit alighting on the person that makes the anointing something significant. The anointing of David and Saul as kings of Israel occurred this way, as can been seen in the Bible in First Samuel.

> Then Samuel took a flask of olive oil and poured it on Saul's head and kissed him, saying, "Has not the LORD anointed you ruler over his inheritance? When you leave me today, . . . you will go to Gibeah of God, where there is a Philistine outpost. As you approach the town, you will meet a procession of prophets coming down from the high place with lyres, timbrels, pipes and harps being played before them, and they will be prophesying. The Spirit of the LORD will come powerfully upon you, and you will prophesy with them; and you will be changed into a different person. . . ." When he and his servant arrived at Gibeah, a procession of prophets met him; the Spirit of God came powerfully upon him, and he joined in their prophesying. (10:1–2, 5–6, 10 NIV)
>
> So Samuel took the horn of oil and anointed him in the presence of his brothers, and from that day on the Spirit of the LORD came upon David in power. Samuel then went to Ramah. (16:13 NIV)

We saw that Jesus said that he was anointed because the Spirit of the Lord was on him. This happened at an earlier time too, as recorded in Luke 3:21–22.

> Now when all the people were baptized, it came to pass, that Jesus also being baptized, and praying, the heaven was opened, And the Holy Ghost descended in a bodily shape like a dove upon him, and a voice came from heaven, which said, Thou art my beloved Son; in thee I am well pleased.

If we have in mind that Jesus was not the first, nor the last person who was crucified by Romans, the question then is what made his death on the cross so significant and important an event for the entire mankind? Looking at the anointing of David and Saul that we just read and relating the spiritual to the physical, we see that exactly what happened on the cross of Christ takes its significant meaning and importance because of the personality that was crucified and also because of the events that happened in the realm of the spirit when Jesus was crucified. Again, remember that the spiritual determines the natural. While on the cross, in the physical realm, Jesus went through some serious sufferings, but in the spiritual unseen realm, these sufferings actually bring and mean tremendous blessings to and for us. For example, on the cross we see that Jesus was physically wounded, while in the spiritual unseen realm the wounds brought us healing. On the cross we see Jesus physically rejected by the Father, while in the spiritual realm it is that rejection that brought us acceptance by the Father.

To summarize, on the cross, Jesus received the evil that should have come to human beings so that human beings could receive the good things that belonged to him (Jesus). Choices usually have their consequences. Sin is a choice to either obey or disobey God. Sin has consequences. Sin opens the door for death and agents of death to enter. If Adam had not sinned, human beings could have lived forever. Sin also opens the door for Satan and his evil spirits to attack the sinner, leaving the footprints of sicknesses, diseases, curses, failures, shame, infirmities, demons, possessions, insanity, addictions, etc.

Let us look at some of these physical things that happened to Jesus on the cross against what happened in the spiritual realm, as well as what they mean and the blessings they bring to those who believe and accept Jesus as Lord. I agree with Derek Prince that the spiritual aspects of what Jesus went through are in perfect harmony with scripture. In his book *The Divine Exchange*, Prince observed several things that Jesus did for mankind when he died on the cross.[6]

a. *Jesus was punished that we might be forgiven.*

> Yet it was our weaknesses he carried; it was our sorrows that weighed him down. And we thought his troubles were a punishment from God, a punishment for his own

---

[6] Derek Prince, *The Divine Exchange* (Charlotte, NC: Derek Prince Ministries, 1995), 26–27, ebook, http://www.derekprince.org/Articles/1000132017/DPM_USA/Contact/Divine_Exchange_form/The_Divine_Exchange.aspx.

sins! But he was pierced for our rebellion, crushed for our sins. He was beaten so we could be whole. He was whipped so we could be healed. All of us, like sheep, have strayed away. We have left God's paths to follow our own. Yet the LORD laid on him the sins of us all. (Isa 53:4–6 NLT)

He had done no wrong and had never deceived anyone. But he was buried like a criminal; he was put in a rich man's grave. But it was the LORD's good plan to crush him and cause him grief. Yet when his life is made an offering for sin, he will have many descendants. He will enjoy a long life, and the LORD's good plan will prosper in his hands. (9–10 NLT)

Verses 4 and 5 summarize the essence of the entire gospel message. All that suffering and pain that should have come to us was put upon Jesus so that God could, and still can, forgive us while maintaining his integrity and holiness. But while Jesus was going through it, we actually thought he was being punished for his own sins.

b. *Jesus was wounded that we might be healed.*

> He personally carried our sins in his body on the cross so that we can be dead to sin and live for what is right. By his wounds you are healed. (1 Pet 2:24 NLT)

Physically, he was wounded but those wounds brought healing to us. He said, this is my body, which is broken for you. The stripes broke the skin (body) to release the healing virtue stored inside his body so that all who believe and receive can be healed.

c. *Jesus was made sin with our sinfulness that we might be made righteous with his righteousness.*

Second Corinthians 5:21 says,

> For He made Him who knew no sin *to be* sin for us, that we might become the righteousness of God in him. (NKJV)
>
> For God made Christ, who never sinned, to be the offering for our sin, so that we could be made right with God through Christ. (NLT)

By becoming our offering for sin, God can also forgive us because a ransom has been paid.

d. *Jesus died our death that we might receive his life.*

> But we see Jesus, who was made a little lower than the angels for the suffering of death, crowned with glory and honour, that he by the grace of God should taste death for every man. (Heb 2:9)

As he died, he released his life to us who would believe as well as accept his sacrifice and offer of pardon. This life is eternal life and those who receive it have both escaped the second death and they will live forever. Friends, Jesus has already tasted and suffered your death for you, why do you want to suffer it again? Why do you want his suffering to be in vain? You can make his suffering count if you accept that he did it for you and if you accept and confess him as your Lord and Savior.

e. *Jesus was made a curse that we might enter into the blessing.*

> Christ hath redeemed us from the curse of the law, being made a curse for us: for it is written, Cursed is every one that hangeth on a tree: That the blessing of Abraham might come on the Gentiles through Jesus Christ; that we might receive the promise of the Spirit through faith. (Gal 3:13–14)

Two themes are clearly taught in the Bible: life and death, and closely associated with them, blessing and cursing. In John 10:10, Jesus said, the thief comes to steal, kill and destroy but he (Jesus) came that we (believers) might have life and have it more abundantly, because in Jesus is life (Johnn1:4), and he is life (John 11:25). The passage in Galatians goes further by saying that not only do we have life (and all it encompasses) in Christ, but also because he took away our curses as he took away sins, the consequences of curses have been removed from us, while blessing and all that accompany blessing have been released upon us (on all who believe and accept Jesus' offer).

f. *Jesus endured our poverty that we might share his abundance.*

> For ye know the grace of our Lord Jesus Christ, that, though he was rich, yet for your sakes he became poor, that ye through his poverty might be rich. (2 Cor 8:9)

Jesus took away poverty and financial lack from us by subjecting himself to all he went through. He did these things in order to meet all the demands of justice, as well as to exhaust the poverty curse (want of all things) so that the curse of poverty is removed from us who believe and we now qualify to partake of his wealth and abundance.

g. *Jesus bore our shame that we might share his glory.*

> And they crucified him, and parted his garments, casting lots: that it might be fulfilled which was spoken by the prophet, They parted my garments among them, and upon my vesture did they cast lots.
>
> And sitting down they watched him there; And set up over his head his accusation written, This Is Jesus the King of The Jews. (Matt 27:35)

They stripped him of his clothes, sat down and watched him hang naked on the cross.

h. *Jesus endured our rejection that we might have his acceptance with the Father.*

Now from the sixth hour there was darkness over all the land unto the ninth hour. And about the ninth hour Jesus cried with a loud voice, saying, Eli, Eli, lama sabachthani? that is to say, My God, my God, why hast thou forsaken me? Some of them that stood there, when they heard that, said, This man calleth for Elias. And straightway one of them ran, and took a sponge, and filled it with vinegar, and put it on a reed, and gave him to drink. The rest said, Let be, let us see whether Elias will come to save him. Jesus, when he had cried again with a loud voice, yielded up the ghost. And, behold, the veil of the temple was rent in twain from the top to the bottom; and the earth did quake, and the rocks rent. (Matt 27:45-51)

Blessed be the God and Father of our Lord Jesus Christ, who hath blessed us with all spiritual blessings in heavenly places in Christ:

According as he hath chosen us in him before the foundation of the world, that we should be holy and without blame before him in love: Having predestinated us unto the adoption of children by Jesus Christ to himself, according to the good pleasure of his will, To the praise of the glory of his grace, wherein he hath made accepted in the beloved. (Eph 1:3-6)

Our rejection was exchanged on the cross so that we can become partakers and heirs of all the spiritual blessings and benefits of predestination in Christ.

HOW DO I GAIN FROM THESE THINGS?

Note that the blessings listed in the previous section are spiritual truths, they are located in the glory realm and we must bring them down into the natural physical realm where we live and where we need them. The way to make these blessings ours is through the confessions we make with our mouth stating our belief in Jesus Christ and what he did for us on the cross. This is also the way to make contact with the spiritual realm through the proclamation of our faith.

> For verily I say unto you, That whosoever shall say unto this mountain, Be thou removed, and be thou cast into the sea; and shall not doubt in his heart, but shall believe that those things which he saith shall come to pass; he shall have whatsoever he saith. (Mark 11:23)

> For with the heart man believeth unto righteousness; and with the mouth confession is made unto salvation. (Rom 10:10)

As we make the confessions, Psalm 103:20 gives us insight into what happens after we have uttered the confession.

> Bless the LORD, ye his angels, that excel in strength, that do his commandments, hearkening unto the voice of his word.

Angels carry out God's commands and obey the voice of his word.

As we confess (speak) the word of God, the angels are immediately prompted to act and bring the word to pass. When we keep quiet, the word of God remains unfulfilled in our lives no matter how committed we are. But as we open our mouths and confess these scriptures that declare what Jesus did and the blessings they confer on us, the angels are prompted to ensure that the word of God comes to pass. If we want these wonderful blessings of Jesus' sacrifice on the cross to be ours, we must give voice to what the Bible says belongs to us before we can experience them physically.

HOW TO USE THE POWER OF JESUS' NAME

The power of the cross of Christ is demonstrated through the confessions of our mouths. As we confess what the Bible says, angels are activated to ensure that what we confess from the Bible (the word of God) comes to pass.

> Wherefore God also hath highly exalted him, and given him a name which is above every name: That at the name of Jesus every knee should bow, of things in heaven, and things in earth, and things under the earth; And that every tongue should confess that Jesus Christ is Lord, to the glory of God the Father. (Phil 2:9–11)

I believe many Christians know that passage of scripture very well and probably know the song from that passage but how many have actually experienced the power of that name in real life? How many actually put the devil to flight using that name? How many have commanded unwanted situations (such as sickness and diseases) to leave in that name?

Let me share a personal experience of putting Philippians 2:10–11 in action to show us that there is real power in that name. This is a true-life story of my encounter with the truth of this scripture. The event happened on a Sunday morning in February of 1999, while I was pastoring RCCG Living Water Parish, then located at 1. Birabi Street, G.R.A Phase 2 in Port Harcourt, Nigeria. During the service that morning, I read a written testimony from the husband of one of our sisters. This sister was diagnosed with hepatitis that had so damaged her liver that the husband was meant to prepare for the funeral service of his wife. But we prayed, God intervened, and miraculously restored her liver to health. At this point, I broke into singing this song:

> His name is higher,
> Than any other name,
> His name is Jesus,
> His name is Lord.
> At the name of Jesus,
> Every knee should bow,
> Every tongue confess that Jesus is Lord . . .

Unbeknownst to me, while we were singing this song, a young man walked into the service and was ushered to a seat at the very point we were singing "at the name of Jesus, every knee should bow." The young man started staggering and falling backward, saying that he was losing his power. The ushers carried him out to one of the rooms, called the prayer team who started praying for him, and observed that each mention of the name of Jesus elicited some reaction from him. This led them to question him and he said he was a servant of the queen of the coast of the occult kingdom of water. He had no assignment that morning and decided to take a walk. Along the way, he observed that there was a completely open, empty space. The young man decided to walk towards the empty space to see what it was all about. The site made him curious, like Moses when he saw a bush burning with fire and the bush was not consumed.

> And the angel of the LORD appeared unto him in a flame of fire out of the midst of a bush: and he looked, and, behold, the bush burned with fire, and the bush was not consumed. And Moses said, I will now turn aside, and see this great sight, why the bush is not burnt. (Exod 3:2–3)

As the young man approached the empty space, he saw our church building and walked towards it. He was ushered into it and then noticed that he started to lose his powers now that he was inside the building. The evil spirits were commanded to leave, and the young man was eventually led to repent and receive Jesus as his Lord and Savior. We then went to his house and destroyed a number of evil paraphernalia.

The lesson I gained from the incident is that the power in the name of Jesus is not visible to the naked eye as it is in the spiritual realm, but it is very potent and effective in dealing with agents of darkness and in determining what we see in the natural physical realm. Pastor E. A. Adeboye reminds us that electricity is not visible to the naked eye either, but it is very potent and produces visible results. We do not have to see it to know that it is active. I am sure there are many believers who have sung that song without even realizing that things happened in the spiritual realm as they sang. May the Lord open your eyes to see one or two things that happen when you mention the name of Jesus in Jesus' name.

The wonderful news about this name that God the Father gave to Jesus is that Jesus gave us the right to use that name here on earth in prayer to God and in dealing with the devil and evil forces of darkness to enforce the victory of the cross. Matthew 28:18–20 says,

> And Jesus came and spake unto them, saying, All power is given unto me in heaven and in earth. Go ye therefore, and teach all nations, baptizing them in the name of the Father, and of the Son, and of the Holy Ghost: Teaching them to observe all things whatsoever I have commanded you: and, lo, I am with you always, even unto the end of the world. Amen.

After Jesus rose from the dead, he told his disciples this wonderful news that all power is given to him in heaven and earth. The word "all" means the whole, the greatest amount possible. Psalm 62:11 says something interesting about power.

> God hath spoken once; twice have I heard this; that power belongeth unto God.

Power belongs to God. And it is described as all power. No wonder Jesus said,

> Behold, I give unto you power to tread on serpents and scorpions, and over all the power of the enemy: and nothing shall by any means hurt you. (Luke 10:19)

The power to tread on serpents and scorpions, and over all the power of the enemy, is one of the signs that shall follow them that believe, as Jesus said,

> In my name shall they cast out devils; they shall speak with new tongues. (Mark 16:17)

In his name you have everything you ask for from the Father. In Jesus' words,

> In that day ye shall ask me nothing. Verily, verily, I say unto you, Whatsoever ye shall ask the Father in my name, he will give it you. Hitherto have ye asked nothing in my name: ask, and ye shall receive, that your joy may be full. (John 16:23)

A man of God described this right to use the name of Jesus in prayer to God as giving us the power of attorney to act on his behalf here on earth, while he is seated on the right hand of the Father in heaven ensuring that what we declare in his name gets done. Power of attorney is a written document given by one person or party to another, authorizing the latter to act for the former. According to Matthew 28:18–20, Jesus gave us the right to use his name on earth and make disciples of all nations. Relating this passage to Mark 16:17–18, where he gave us the right to use his name and act on his behalf on earth, we find that he gave us the power of attorney. From the definition of the power of attorney, we conclude that Jesus gave us the right to act on his behalf here on earth after he had gone back to heaven. Because that name has power in heaven, the Bible says, angels hearken to the voice of the word of God.

> Bless the LORD, ye his angels that excel in strength, that do his commandments, hearkening unto the voice of his word. (Ps 103:20)

And Hebrews 1:13–14 says the angels are to minister (serve) us, the heirs of salvation.

> But to which of the angels said he at any time, Sit on my right hand, until I make thine enemies thy footstool? Are they not all ministering spirits, sent forth to minister for them who shall be heirs of salvation?

When we issue a command or make demands on the agents of darkness in the name of Jesus, the angels are triggered to go and ensure that what we decree in that name comes to pass.

According to John 8:34, before we got saved, because of Adam's sin, we were slaves of sin and Satan. Satan and his agents could oppress us; they could disturb us anyhow, anytime, and anywhere. Satan and his demons had the legal right to violate anyone in their sleep at night. A number of people have sex in their sleep at night (often called wet dreams). When they awaken, they feel like it was a dream that they remember clearly. Others experience oppression in their sleep at night in which they have the feeling or dream that something is pressing down on them and they are unable to fight it.

Now, we must understand that not everybody experiences these dreams. Though all were under the power of Satan and sin before Jesus came, all do not experience satanic oppression equally. Some experience it more than others. There are many people all over the world who have never experienced having sex in their dreams whereas to some others, it is a major problem from which they seek deliverance. No matter who or what level of subjection, there is deliverance for all from satanic oppression and dreams through Jesus and what he did on the cross.

> Who hath delivered us from the power of darkness, and hath translated us into the kingdom of his dear Son. (Col 1:13)

Jesus delivered us from the dominion of darkness; from the power of poverty and shame, and sickness and diseases, and so much more. Now, dominion means the power or right of governing and controlling. So Jesus delivered us from under the control of Satan and agents of darkness. Jesus made us free—absolutely free.

> And ye shall know the truth, and the truth shall make you free. They answered him, We be Abraham's seed, and were never in bondage to any man: how sayest thou, Ye shall be made free? Jesus answered them, Verily, verily, I say unto you, Whosoever committeth sin is the servant of sin. And the servant abideth not in the house for ever: but the Son abideth ever. If the Son therefore shall make you free, ye shall be free indeed. (John 8:32–36)

Because on the cross, Jesus was our substitute, and he did it publicly, anyone who publicly comes to Jesus and confesses him as Lord is instantly translated from under the dominion of darkness to the dominion of light and power of God. Here, under the power and dominion of God, no one can touch or disturb you at will; neither can they oppress you in your sleep at night. They are not allowed to place sickness on you. They can no longer place you under a curse nor can they shame you, keep you poor, or make you miscarry, etc. When you know this and stand your ground against them in the name of Jesus, you demonstrate the power of the cross. When you preach the gospel, and sinners come to trust in, receive, and confess Jesus as their Lord and Savior, you demonstrate the power of the cross.

Remember what Paul said in our main text, 1 Corinthians 1:17–18:

> For Christ sent me not to baptize, but to preach the gospel: not with wisdom of words, lest the cross of Christ should be made of none effect. For the preaching of the cross is to them that perish foolishness; but unto us which are saved it is the power of God.

Paul said in another passage that the Gospel message is the power of God unto salvation.

> For I am not ashamed of the gospel of Christ: for it is the power of God unto salvation to everyone that believeth; to the Jew first, and also to the Greek (Rom 1:16).

When you preach the gospel, you demonstrate that power as you see souls delivered from the dominion of Satan and darkness, you watch people come forward to put their faith and trust in Jesus as Lord and Savior. Whenever you use his name to enforce the victory of the cross you demonstrate the power of the cross. You enforce the defeat of the kingdom of darkness over your life, health, family, ministry, business, finances, and everything else.

When you declare with your mouth, for example, "Satan, I command you in the name of Jesus, lift your hands off my finances. Holy Angels of God, I command you in the name of Jesus, go forth into the four corners of the earth and wherever my finances have been held down, loose them and bring them to me in Jesus' name," it gets done. When sickness attacks your body and you stand your ground and resist the sickness in the name of Jesus and say, for example, "I refuse to allow sickness to stay on my body; therefore, in the name of Jesus, I resist every attack of sickness. I confess that my body is the temple of the Holy Ghost and sickness is not allowed in my body. I come against every attempt to place sickness on my body in the name of Jesus. I cast that fever out of my body in Jesus' name. I command the spirit behind hypertension or diabetes or leukemia (mention the name of the affliction) to leave my body now in Jesus' name." When you pray in Jesus's name, know that it gets done. Quote scripture (so that angels are triggered to enforce it). For example, in cases where you need healing, take a scripture such as 1 Peter 2:24, "Who his own self bare our sins in his own body on the tree, that we, being dead to sins, should live unto righteousness: by whose stripes ye were healed," and make it more personal. You could say, "On the cross, Jesus himself bore my sins on his own body on the tree that I being dead to sins should live for righteousness, by whose stripes (wounds), I was healed." Keep praying, "Therefore I am healed and these symptoms of sickness cannot continue as I walk by faith (in the word of God) not by what I feel or see."

As you make these confessions in line with the Bible (word of God), angels enforce the commands you issue and the symptoms eventually disappear. What I cannot tell you is how long it will take for them to disappear, but keep at it and it will happen. The Bible says you will have what you say.

> For verily I say unto you, That whosoever shall say unto this mountain, Be thou removed, and be thou cast into the sea; and shall not doubt in his heart, but shall believe that those things which he saith shall come to pass; he shall have whatsoever he saith. (Mark 11:23)

Once you make your confessions, you must then continually maintain them. When you refuse to allow anything contrary to the word of God to come out of your mouth, this is maintaining your confession. By doing all of this, you demonstrate the power of the cross of Christ through his name. When you lay hands on those who are sick and command them to be healed in Jesus' name, you demonstrate the power of the cross of Christ.

> Now Peter and John went up together into the temple at the hour of prayer, being the ninth hour. And a certain man lame from his mother's womb was carried, whom they laid daily at the gate of the temple which is called Beautiful, to ask alms of them that entered into the temple; Who seeing Peter and John about to go into the temple asked an alms. And Peter, fastening his eyes upon him with John, said, Look on us. And he gave heed unto them, expecting to receive something of them. Then Peter said, Silver and gold have I none; but such as I have give I thee: In the name of Jesus Christ of Nazareth rise up and walk. And he took him by the right hand, and lifted him up: and immediately his feet and ankle bones received strength. And he leaping up stood, and walked, and entered with them into the temple, walking, and leaping, and praising God. And all the people saw him walking and praising God. (Acts 3:1–9)

Peter and John recalled what Jesus told them.

> And whatsoever ye shall ask in my name, that will I do, that the Father may be glorified in the Son. If ye shall ask any thing in my name, I will do it. (John 14:13–14)

They put it to work by acting on it, made a demand on Satan (to lose his hold on the man's legs) and on the name of Jesus (to ensure that what they said got done) and they received the result they expected. Observe that Peter and John could have given the man the money he asked for or walked on without a care (as most of us do when faced with such scenarios where a lame man asks for money). If they had walked away, they would not have gotten the result they got and we would not have that evidence recorded in scripture for us. We may never know what power of the cross can be demonstrated when we use the name of Jesus to confront unpleasant situations such as lameness, blindness, barrenness, sickness, lack, insufficiency, poverty, etc.

Chapter 6

HOW CAN YOU CLAIM THE POWER OF THE CROSS?

We have seen that the cross of Jesus Christ is a real event in the history of man. The significance of the cross is as a result of the personality involved, (God in the person of Jesus Christ) as well as the spiritual (unseen) happenings that took place (*pari passu*) as he died physically on the cross. Jesus' death on the cross paved the way for you, for me, and all of mankind to have eternal life. So how can we gain access to this incredible gift? Salvation is what qualifies you to benefit from the power of the cross, and to enter heaven; it takes you out of Satan's domain and makes you a child of God.

> As many as received him, to them gave he power to become the sons of God, even to them that believe on his name. Salvation seats you and I with Christ in Heavenly places. (John 1:12)
>
> But God, who is rich in mercy, for his great love wherewith he loved us, Even when we were dead in sins, hath quickened us together with Christ, (by grace ye are saved;) And hath raised us up together, and made us sit together in heavenly places in Christ Jesus. (Eph 2:4–6)

Know who you are in Christ and your right in him under the New Testament. This is important, because knowledge of who you are in Christ will determine the way you use the authority you have in him to attack the kingdom of darkness and establish God's kingdom here on earth. Recognize and use the authority bestowed on you to use the name of Jesus in prayer to God and receive answers to your prayers. Recognize your right to use the name of Jesus to resist and put a stop to the activities of the kingdom of darkness over your own life, health, family, business, church, and nation.

But remember, unless you have been delivered from the power of sin, and exercise your rights and privileges as a child of God, you will continue to be bound by the devil and his agents.

> He that committeth sin is of the devil; for the devil sinneth from the beginning. For this purpose the Son of God was manifested, that he might destroy the works of the devil. (1 John 3:8)

> How God anointed Jesus of Nazareth with the Holy Ghost and with power: who went about doing good, and healing all that were oppressed of the devil; for God was with him. (Acts 10:38)

Jesus destroyed the works of the devil because God anointed him and was with him. He in turn sent us and is with us as we use his name to put a stop to the activities of the devil and the entire kingdom of darkness. Remember that he is with you always as shown in the Bible.

> Teaching them to observe all things whatsoever I have commanded you: and, lo, I am with you always, even unto the end of the world. Amen. (Matt 28:20)

> And they went forth, and preached everywhere, the Lord working with them, and confirming the word with signs following. Amen. (Mark 16:20)

STEPS TO SALVATION

What are the steps you need to take in order to be saved, to become God's child and remain one? First of all, acknowledge that you are a sinner, you were born in sin, and need a Savior. The Bible assures us of this fact; it is spelled out very clearly in the book of Romans.

> For all have sinned, and come short of the glory of God. (3:23)
>
> Wherefore, as by one man sin entered into the world, and death by sin; and so death passed upon all men, for that all have sinned. (5:12)
>
> For the wages of sin is death; but the gift of God is eternal life through Jesus Christ our Lord. (6:23)

Second, recognize that God sent his son Jesus Christ who was born of a virgin and lived without sin but died for all sinners on the cross at Calvary. He was buried and rose from the dead after three days. Scripture says,

> For God so loved the world, that he gave his only begotten Son, that whosoever believeth in him should not perish, but have everlasting life. (John 3:16)
>
> Who was delivered for our offenses, and was raised because of our justification. (Rom 4:25)

Third, repent of your sins, confess and receive Jesus as your Lord and Savior. You do not need fancy words, you just need to speak from your heart when you repent and confess before God.

> That if thou shalt confess with thy mouth the Lord Jesus, and shalt believe in thine heart that God hath raised him from the dead, thou shalt be saved. (Rom 10:9)

Fourth, endeavor to read the Bible every day. First Peter 2:2 (NASB) says, "like newborn babies, long for the pure milk of the word, so that by it you may grow in respect to salvation."

Fifth, join a Bible-believing church and grow in your new faith and relationship with your heavenly Father through Jesus Christ his son. Make every effort to stay away from sin, but when you do sin, immediately confess the sin and repent of it in the name of Jesus. See 1 John 1:7 and 9.

> But if we walk in the light, as he is in the light, we have fellowship one with another, and the blood of Jesus Christ his Son cleanseth us from all sin. (7)
>
> If we confess our sins, he is faithful and just to forgive us our sins, and to cleanse us from all unrighteousness. (9)

Sixth, live a life of continuous thanksgiving to God for the salvation of your soul.

> By him therefore let us offer the sacrifice of praise to God continually, that is, the fruit of our lips giving thanks to his name. (Heb 13:15)

PRAYER FOR SALVATION

Finally, do you want to receive this gift of pardon that Jesus purchased for you on the cross? If you want to repent of your sin and receive Jesus as your Lord and Savior, pray the following prayer out loud and mean what you say with your heart:

> Heavenly Father, I come to you in the name of Jesus. I confess that I am a sinner and I cannot save myself from my sins. But because you love me, you sent Jesus Christ your only begotten son to die for my sins, and you raised him from the dead on the third day.
>
> Lord Jesus, I repent of my sins and surrender my life to you as I invite you into my heart. Come and be my Lord and Savior. I believe that you died on the cross, and you were buried and rose from the dead after three days.

> I believe with my heart in the Lord Jesus and I confess with my mouth that God has raised him from the dead. Therefore, I am saved. Thank you Heavenly Father for saving me in Jesus' name.

If you said that prayer, congratulations, you are born again and the power of the cross of Christ just manifested in you. Welcome into the family of God, your name is now written in the book of life in heaven.

You will need to look for a Bible-believing church near where you live, go and introduce yourself to the pastor, and let him or her know you just prayed the prayer to receive Jesus as your Savior. Enroll in the baptismal class and quickly get baptized by water immersion and continue to attend and participate in all the church services. If you do these things you will continue to grow in grace and in the knowledge of Jesus until he returns.

God bless you and see you in heaven. Hallelujah, Jesus is alive and he is Lord forever.

www.ingramcontent.com/pod-product-compliance
Lightning Source LLC
LaVergne TN
LVHW011210080426
835508LV00007B/707